John Matthews

# *the grail*

## Quest for the eternal

with 118 illustrations, 15 in color

Thames and Hudson

For Caitlín

I should like to thank all those who helped me, one way or the other, in the completion of this book; especially Brian Cleeve, August Closs, Gareth Knight, T.M., Caitlín Matthews, Jill Purce, Peter Lamborn Wilson, Grahaeme Young, Elémire Zolla; and all those who, known and unknown, keep alive the fellowship of the Grail.

ART AND IMAGINATION
General Editor: Jill Purce

First published in the United States in 1991 by Thames and Hudson Inc., 500 Fifth Avenue New York, New York 10110

Library of Congress Catalog Card Number 90-71439

Filmset in Great Britain by Keyspools Ltd, Golborne, Lancashire
Printed and bound in Japan by Dai Nippon

# Contents

*Here is the Book of thy Descent,*
*Here begins the Book of the Sangreal,*
*Here begin the terrors,*
*Here begin the miracles.*

*Perlesvaus*

# Quest for the eternal

The symbol of the Grail has occupied a place in the imagination since awareness of it first dawned in the European Middle Ages; and it continues to exert a fascination upon all who come within its sphere of influence. Yet there is no single, clearly defined image of the Grail, nor indeed evidence that it ever existed; opinions differ widely about the origins of the stories that have circulated in written form since the beginning of the twelfth century. Its outward shape is debated – it may be a cup, a shallow dish, a stone or a jewel – yet most agree that it is a profound and mysterious thing, perhaps worth giving up the whole of one's life to find, even in the knowledge that the search may be fruitless.

It was this quest that dominated the stories of the Grail throughout the Middle Ages, and no matter what form the quest took, the objective remained the same: a spiritual goal representing inner wholeness, union with the divine, self-fulfilment. The scene is usually set in a far-off country of Paradisial status, where the Grail is housed in a temple on top of a mountain, surrounded by water and protected by obstacles which only the chosen few can overcome. Its guardian is both a priest and a king, at once alive and dead; and the rewards of the hero successful in the quest are good fortune, blessings and (sometimes) the hand of the king's daughter.

These elements are the basic matter of the story, and are to be found, in varying forms, in a world-wide mythological context, by no means always Christian – for though the Grail became firmly entrenched in the western imagination as a symbol of Christ's teaching, it can be shown that a considerable amount of the imagery originated in eastern cultures. But before we can begin to separate the many strands that constitute the life of the symbol, it is necessary to remind ourselves of the story as it has come down to us by way of the mediaeval texts. They tell us almost all we know of the Grail's outward history, and it is from them that the following narrative is reconstructed.

The story begins with Joseph of Arimathaea, a wealthy Jew to whose care Christ's body is given for burial and who, according to some stories, also obtains the cup used by Christ at the Last Supper. While he is washing the body to prepare it for the tomb, some blood flows from the wounds which he catches in this vessel. After the disappearance of the body, Joseph is accused of stealing it, is thrown into prison and deprived of food. Here

Christ appears to him in a blaze of light and entrusts the cup to his care. He then instructs Joseph in the mystery of the Mass and, it is said, certain other secrets, before vanishing. Joseph is miraculously kept alive by a dove which enters his cell every day and deposits a wafer in the cup. He is released in AD 70 and, joined by his sister and her husband Bron, goes into exile overseas with a small group of followers. A table called the First Table of the Grail is constructed, to represent the Table of the Last Supper (a fish is laid in Christ's place) at which twelve may sit down. A thirteenth seat, representing the place of Judas, remains empty after one of the company tries to sit in it and is swallowed up. (This seat is thereafter referred to as the Siege Perilous.)

According to some versions, Joseph then sails to Britain, where he sets up the first Christian church at Glastonbury, dedicating it to the Mother of Christ. Here the Grail is housed, and serves as a chalice at the celebration of the Mass in which the whole company participate, and which becomes known as the Mass of the Grail.

In other versions Joseph goes no further than Europe, and the guardianship of the cup passes to Bron, who becomes known as the Rich Fisher after he miraculously feeds the company from it with a single fish, echoing Christ's feeding of the five thousand. The company settles at a place called Avaron (perhaps the same as Avalon, the Celtic name for the Otherworld, also identified with Glastonbury) to await the coming of the third Grail Keeper, Alain.

A temple is built on Muntsalvach, the Mountain of Salvation, to house the vessel, and an Order of Grail Knights comes into being. They sit at a Second Table, and partake of a sacred feast provided by the Grail; a form of Mass also takes place at which the Grail Keeper, now called King, serves as priest. Shortly after, he receives a mysterious wound, variously said to be in the thighs or the genitals, caused by a spear and attributed to one of several different causes, among which are the loss of faith, the love of a woman against a vow of chastity, or an accidental blow struck by a stranger in self-defence. Hereafter the guardian is known as the Maimed or Wounded King, and the country around the Grail castle becomes barren and is called the Waste Land – a state explicitly connected with the Grail King's wound. The spear with which he is struck becomes identified with the Lance of Longinus, the Roman soldier who in Biblical tradition pierced the side of Christ on the cross. This spear, the Grail, a sword and a dish-shaped platter (which in more primitive versions of the story may have borne a human head, and which later becomes confused with the Grail itself) constitute the objects, called Hallows, to be found in the Grail castle.

By this time we have reached the age of Arthur, and the scene is set for the beginning of the quest. The Round Table is established by Merlin the enchanter as the Third Table (from which the Grail itself is, however, absent) and a fellowship of knights led by Arthur meet around it, bound by the rules of chivalry. At Pentecost the Grail makes an appearance, floating veiled in a beam of sunlight, and the knights pledge themselves to go in search of it. There follow a series of initiatory adventures involving most of the fellowship, especially Lancelot, Gawaine and Bors. Two others – Perceval (Parzival or Parsifal), nicknamed the Perfect Fool in token of his innocence, and Lancelot's son Galahad, who is from the beginning singled out for

special significance by being permitted to sit unscathed in the Siege Perilous – are given particular emphasis, their adventures forming the greater part of the narrative from this point.

Of the many who set out from the Arthurian court at Camelot, few catch more than a glimpse of the elusive Grail. A series of tests are set for each knight, and their nature explained by a succession of hermit figures who are always at hand in the deep wood where the questers often find themselves. Lancelot comes agonizingly close to the holy vessel, but is turned away, temporarily blinded, because of his adulterous love for Arthur's queen. Gawaine reaches the Grail castle, but fails as it is his nature to fail, being too much in the world and without the simplicity or the spiritual qualities required of the true quester.

Only three succeed in finding the Grail and participating, to varying degrees, in its mystery. They are Galahad, the stainless, virgin knight, Perceval, the holy fool, and Bors, the humble, 'ordinary' man, who is the only one of the three to return to Camelot with news of the quest. Perceval, after first failing and wandering for five years in the wilderness, finds his way again to the castle of the Wounded King (who is sometimes his uncle, as well as the Fisher King, the guardian of the way to the Waste Land) and by asking a ritual question – usually, 'Whom does the Grail serve?' – brings about his healing. (The answer, never explicitly stated, is the King himself, who is kept alive, though in torment from his wound, beyond his normal life-span.) Once healed, the King is permitted to·die, and the waters of the Waste Land flow again, making it flower. Galahad, Perceval and Bors continue their journey, eventually reaching Ṣarras (perhaps a corruption of Muntsalvach) the Heavenly City in the East, where the final mysteries of the Grail are celebrated and where the three knights take part in a Mass in which the vessel is again used as the chalice; Christ appears first as celebrant and then as a radiant child and finally, in the Host, as a crucified man. After this, Galahad dies in an odour of sanctity and the Grail is taken up into heaven: Perceval goes back to the Fisher King's castle to rule in his place, leaving Bors to return alone to Camelot. (For a list of Grail texts, see p.96.)

Given the length of time – about 150 years – which spans the formation of this story, it is amazing that such a consistent body of myths should have evolved around the symbol. Origin, history, development and final disappearance are there in detail, and though there are contradictions in the form taken by the vessel, there are few in the history of its time in the world. And this is an important clue to the nature of the Grail as a symbol, and to how it was understood by those who told of its existence. At no time, however, did the established Church make any reference to what was clearly an important and widely recognized object, either to confirm or to deny its existence. This, in an age of relic hunting, is more than just unusual.

Why did the Church Fathers keep silent? It may have been because they knew that the Grail was associated by some with heresy, and that there may even have been an attempt to form a second Church with the Grail as its central symbol. Or they may have recognized the borrowings to be from other, non-Christian sources. Whatever the reason, they maintained their silence. This may have helped to foster the image of a secret cult of the Grail, but the fact that they did not denounce it prevented it from becoming the cause of speculation. Perhaps they believed that, with the stamping out of the Cathar heresy in Southern France (with which, as we shall see, the Grail had strong links), the matter would die out on its own. Its refusal to do so is evidenced by the continuing strength of the tradition. Yet its origins remain obscure, confused by the many different interpretations to which the symbol has been subject. At the beginning of the twelfth century hardly anyone had heard of the Grail; by the end of the thirteenth there could be few who had not. Yet the literature of the holy vessel occurred with such apparent suddenness that one can only assume it was giving shape to an already well defined body of oral myths. The reasons for this become apparent only when the symbol is viewed in a broader spectrum: by considering the history of the sacred vessel as a symbol, of which the Grail was only the latest manifestation.

## The legend: its origins and development

The symbol of the sacred vessel as an object of power and as the cause of miraculous events is at least as old as history. It stems from the roots of the human psyche and appears in the earliest shapes painted on cave walls by the first men. Behind it lies the concept of the circle, which can contain all being: life itself, in its circular journey from birth to death. Perhaps this concept is the basis too for the 'cup and ring' markings traced on standing stones and burial mounds throughout the ancient world, made by the same people who constructed their graves in the shape of a reclining woman through whose womb they would enter at death (as in the prehistoric houses of Malta), and their temples in the form of a circle. From the earliest times, people have seen the sky as an upturned bowl covering the earth, and the sun and moon as filled with liquors of the gods. Sometimes, heroes partook of these divine beverages served in rich vessels, thereby endowing themselves with untold strength and endless life, often after a quest involving supernatural adventures and encounters with the gods and goddesses within whose realm these objects lay. Or else the gods themselves were seen to perform miracles with them, like those done, long after, in the name of the Grail. An instance of this is the story of the Vedic god Indra, who stole the fire of the sun and the divine drink, Soma, from the moon, and who carried a spear with which he brought fertility to the dry land. In the Grail stories the lance or spear was of particular significance, and Indra's action, a 'freeing of the waters', is like that of Perceval, who, when he heals the Wounded King, causes streams and rivers to flow again. It is also believed that when the Vedic peoples inhabited a colder region of the world, Indra was known as the god who caused the thaw and brought spring, which may help to explain why, in one version, the Grail King's wound, healed by the touch of the spear, is said to have been made more unendurable by the frost which gripped the land (see Closs).

In Greek philosophy, the idea of the vessel was present in the form of the *Krater* or cup, which stood for the matrix of creation, the divine mixing-bowl into which the deity poured the elements of life, and which was offered to newly created souls that they might imbibe intelligence and wisdom. Plato mentions a Vulcan *Krater*, a fiery cup in which was mixed the light of the sun, and in his *Psychogony* refers to two other vessels, in one of which the deity mixed 'the All-Soul of Universal Nature' and from the other 'ladled out the minds of men'. Elsewhere, Plato says that through drinking from the *Krater* 'the Soul is dragged back into a body, hurried on by new intoxication, desiring to taste a fresh draught of the overflow of Matter, whereby it is weighed down and brought back to earth'. (See Mead, esp. pp. 106–07.)

G. R. S. Mead, in his study of the Orphic mysteries, relates these vessels to the cup of Dionysos, from which inspiration came, and says that Orpheus 'ranges many other such cups around the Solar Table', which according to Orphic cosmology was the centre and beginning of the universe. Mead adds that this means that 'the various spheres were each in turn cups containing the essence (of Creation)'. So that here we have a vessel conceived as a cosmic container and as a prefiguring of the Round Table at which the Grail was later to appear.

To the Celtic races the vessel was the Cauldron – of Rebirth, of Inspiration, or of Plenty – and as such it was a familiar concept. Hell itself (*Annwn*) had such a vessel, in which the dead, dipped head first, were returned to life, though bereft of speech. Arthur himself, who appears in an early version of the Grail story in a more heroic guise, was said to have gone in search of it – entering the 'Fortress of the Turning Door' where it was kept; just as the Grail King Nasciens, who also figures in the earlier stories, finds himself carried by invisible hands to a 'turning island' where the Grail appears to him. Like his knights in later versions, Arthur and his men apparently returned empty handed, and somewhat reduced in numbers: 'Except seven, none returned from Caer Siddi', says the poem 'Preiddeu Annwn' (The Spoils of Annwn), which tells the story.

Other owners of magical or wonder-working vessels in Celtic sources include the Irish Dagda, or Father of the Gods, who possesses a cauldron which will only cook food for a hero – 'The food of a coward would never be in it' – and which, like the Grail, serves food to an assembly of warriors. In Wales, the gods Brân the Blessed and Matholwych possessed similar objects; while another figure, Gwyddno Garanhir, owned a basket which, if filled with enough food for one, on being opened would be found to contain enough for a hundred. Of these three, Brân is an early type of Wounded King, struck with a spear which causes a wound which does not heal; and his name is echoed by that of Bron, the Rich Fisher. Another, even more famous cauldron belonged to the Welsh goddess Ceridwen, in which she brewed a dark drink for her malformed son Avagddu, to instil him with knowledge. By chance it was Gwion Bach, her servant, who, while he was stirring the cauldron, tasted three drops that fell onto his hand. After a series of metamorphoses into animal forms, he was finally reborn as Taliesin ('The Radiant Brow'), and became 'Chief Bard of the Island of Britain', possessing all knowledge through the agency of the cauldron.

It is possible to see behind the story of Taliesin echoes of a mystery religion in which a sacred vessel played an important part – perhaps like the ritual depicted on the walls of the Villa of the Mysteries at Pompeii (second century AD), where the initiate was offered a cup prior to undergoing tests which, if successfully completed, would impart to him the tenets of the inner life. Perhaps Taliesin was given such a drink, and what follows is a symbolic description of the journey towards initiation.

This initiation process occurs again in the Eleusinian mysteries. As well as a mystical feast echoing that partaken of by the Grail knights, there was a sacred vessel, the *Kernos*, which contained an initiatory drink, and whose form was that of a central bowl with several smaller cups attached to it. These were supposed to contain the essential ingredients of the sacred drink, a concept very like that of the Greek *Krater* already discussed. (See Wasson.)

At Eleusis, as in most other mystery religions, the keynote was of passage, during a trance, from this world into another, Paradisial sphere, in which lay delight and healing for the soul, hitherto divided by its sojourn in the physical world.

It is here, perhaps, that the second great strand in the history of the Grail comes into being. For behind the mediaeval stories lie not only the ancient myths of the rape of the sun vessel, as in the story of Indra, or the creation of the cosmos in the *Krater* of the gods, not only the search for knowledge and truth, but also the eternal quest for Paradise, where all secrets will be revealed and the pains and sorrows of life washed away. The Grail, the Cauldron of Ceridwen, the *Krater*, and the bowl and cups of the Orphic and Eleusinian mysteries, were all gateways to Paradise, whether Christian or pagan; and it was in Paradise that they were to be found.

An amalgam of many things gave rise to the symbol of the Grail. Traces of alchemical lore and classical myth, of Arabic poetry and Sufi teaching, of Celtic mythology and Christian iconography are all to be found in the final image. There is no single avenue of transmission. The most satisfactory explanation of its development is that the ancient symbol of the vessel, and the myths and legends which surrounded it, coalesced around the Christian image of the chalice, and through that with the cup of the Last Supper.

This is borne out by the earliest Grail text to have survived, Chrétien de Troyes' *Conte del Graal*, composed towards the end of the twelfth century. Here we have the theme of quest, the adventure which leads to the castle of the Wounded King, where a procession of youths and maidens carries an object called a *graal* (literally, dish) through the hall. Nothing more is told of it than this. It is certainly *not* a holy relic, and there is no mention of Christ's blood or of the Mass. But Chrétien left the story unfinished when he died, and the mystery to be solved by a succession of followers who wrote 'continuations' of the *Conte*, always adding and elaborating until the various endings ran to several times the length of the original story.

Robert de Borron was the next writer to add significantly to the corpus, and by the time his *Joseph d'Arimathie* ('Joseph of Arimathaea'), the first of a projected trilogy, appeared in about 1190, the Grail had become firmly identified as the cup of the Last Supper and the vessel in which Christ's blood had been caught. De Borron (who despite his name was English) seems to have drawn on the Apocryphal 'Gospel of Nicodemus' and 'Acts of Pilate' for much of his material, in particular for the events concerning the imprisonment of Joseph, his miraculous survival, and his departure to spread the teachings of Christ abroad. There already seems to have existed a tradition which credited Joseph with the possession of certain teachings not made available even to the Apostles; and a suspicion that he may have been expelled from the Christianized Roman Empire of Vespasian for attempting to teach these mysteries. This may even be the real reason for the Church's later silence about the Grail. As the temporal power of the Church was given into the hands of Peter, so the spiritual nature of Christ's teachings became enshrined in the cup that was given to Joseph. It was known that he had come west to Britain and had founded a church at Glastonbury dedicated to the Virgin Mary. But by the time the Grail romances were being written, Mary herself had been drawn into the story, and there may have been many willing to believe in a 'Secret Church of the Grail', founded by Joseph and continuing to flourish alongside the established Church.

With De Borron the theme of the story changed; no longer was the object of the quest merely to heal the Wounded King and the Waste Land; a fascination with the blood *in* the cup led away from the Fisher King, now symbolically identified with Christ, towards the cup of the Passion.

In the mediaeval mind, Christ's blood contained both the 'soul', and possibly even the Divinity of the Saviour. It possessed unlimited powers of healing, and it was a means of transmitting a *direct apprehension* of God. A spiritual essence, and one which was beyond price. Illustrations exist which show the heart of Christ, marked with the stigmata of His five wounds, letting forth blood and water; the blood, which being symbolically shed 'for all men', was also seen as an individual life-giving source. Other iconographical sources represent Christ in the wine press, recalling His statement 'I am the True Vine', and depicting the blood spurting forth to feed the multitude of Christian believers. When one realizes that behind the word 'Sangreal', used by the later romancers, lie the words 'Saint Gréal' (Holy Grail) and 'Sang Real' (Royal Blood), one can see how easily the life-giving properties of the blood could be extended to include the cup in which it had been carried.

This may well account for the association of the Grail with the chalice of the Mass; and it is interesting that it was during the period when the Grail was most active in people's imagination, that the Host, hitherto kept hidden during the celebration of the Eucharist, was first openly elevated. It is almost as though one mystery replaced the other, that when the secret of the Mass was made open to all, the Grail took its place as a more profound celebration. Nor should we forget the custom, also current, of reserving the Host – previously blessed and kept in a special container – for later distribution in private houses and castles where there was no resident priest. The element of wonder – the closed box, perhaps made of precious metal and kept in a lonely castle – could have recalled the stories of the Grail. (See Every, pp. 96–97.)

Robert de Borron claimed that his *Joseph* had been given to him by an angel, or even by Christ Himself, in the form of a book which later disappeared; and, by this claim to divine inspiration, established an aura of authenticity in his work and strengthened its links with Christian dogma. But it was the writers of the great compilation known as the *Queste del Saint Graal* ('The Vulgate Cycle'), finished in 1210, who completed the transformation from the mysterious object introduced by Chrétien into a fully fledged Christian symbol.

Chronicling the history of the Grail from Joseph of Arimathaea to its final departure for Sarras and beyond, the compilers of the *Queste* – probably Cistercian clerks from one of the large monasteries in France – patiently interpreted the symbolism of the Grail in the language and terminology of the Church. They also brought onto the scene a new character.

Probably one of the most important events in the literary history of the Grail was the creation of Galahad, the virgin knight destined from birth to achieve the quest. Before him, Perceval represented the ordinary man's search for the supreme mystery; but Galahad is far from being an ordinary man – indeed he scarcely seems like a human being at all, so total is his spirituality. He lives on the borderland between the earthly and the divine, and is in some senses a bridge between this world and the next. Lancelot, his father, is the Best Knight in the World, the perfect representation of the chivalric ideal; yet Lancelot is flawed, because he loves his lord's wife. He is the product of *Amour Courtois* – Courtly Love.

Courtly Love has its place in the history of the Grail for several reasons. As a civilizing force, it drew inspiration from women, hitherto virtually ignored in the culture of the Middle Ages. Drawing freely on the sentiments expressed in Arabic poetry and song, as well as on the teachings of the Sufi mystics whose beliefs included idealized earthly love as a means to spiritual perfection, Courtly Love placed woman on a pedestal for the first time in that age, worshipped her as a goddess, revered her as an almost sacred object of devotion – and in so doing touched off a spark in the poetic consciousness which resulted in a flood of lyricism and song. The Troubadours, singers and poets who celebrated the art of Courtly Love in all its aspects, became a dominant force in western culture. Love became a faith to live by, a code second only to that of chivalry, with which it was closely linked. A complex set of laws ruled every act of courtship made by the knight for love of his lady, who was always portrayed as aloof, cold of heart and lacking in charity, and who humbled her worshipper with cruel words, only spurring him on to greater efforts to please her. Though never

*Galahad prays before the altar of the Grail while Bors rests near by. (Manuscript illustration, France, 15th c.)*

classed as a heresy, Courtly Love was clearly frowned upon by the Church, especially because of the rule contained in it which decreed that the most perfect relationship between a knight and a lady was when the lady was already married. Chrétien de Troyes' most famous work before the *Conte del Graal* was a long poem called *The Knight of the Cart*, which introduced Lancelot as a major figure in the Arthurian Cycle and made him the lover of Queen Guinevere – not only the wife of Arthur, but a perfect type of Courtly lady.

One of the authors of the *Queste* decided that Lancelot's sin should be redeemed at the cost of his personal failure in the quest for the Grail. In the *Queste*, Lancelot is tricked into making love to the Grail King's daughter, because he thinks she is Guinevere. The result is the birth of Galahad, the Perfect Knight in both the spiritual and temporal sense. From Lancelot's sin is born the one who will achieve the Grail and redeem the Waste Land; the virgin knight who will have nothing to do with women – the Courtly ethic reversed. Lancelot is reborn in his son as spiritually superior man, and from this moment the Grail myth is inextricably bound up with the idea of redemption. Galahad becomes a symbol of Christ as man, as distinct from Christ as saviour, symbolized by the Grail.

After this, though many more texts were to be written, most were little more than reworkings or compilations of the original material. The basic pattern had been laid down; and of the three major works that remain to be discussed, only one added significantly to the shape of the stories.

This work, completed by 1207, is the *Parzival* of Wolfram von Eschenbach, and it displays the most individual and personal approach to the Grail myth yet. Wolfram is the most consistent and obvious borrower from eastern sources, to which he clearly had considerable access; and he was a mystic who possessed a remarkable insight into the nature of the Grail. We shall look at his work more fully in the context of its references to alchemy.

The only really significant mediaeval texts to succeed Wolfram were the anonymous *Perlesvaus* (c.1225), and Sir Thomas Malory's *Morte d'Arthur*, printed by Caxton in 1485. *Perlesvaus* reaches an extreme of Christian mysticism not attained even by the *Queste*, and demands a more thorough study than it has yet received. In particular there is the mysterious statement that the Grail undergoes five changes of shape, of which only the fifth, a chalice, is named. Malory, who is the last of the true mediaeval romancers, wrote what is probably the most famous Arthurian work; but his concerns were different to those of his predecessors, his interests more with the code of chivalry than with the mysticism of the Grail. His *Book of the Sangreal*, though finely written, is little more than a parade of half-understood symbols. The drama has passed to the human characters; it is the failure of Lancelot we remember, rather than the success of Galahad.

With Malory, the literary history of the Grail was virtually at an end. From the dawn of the Renaissance onwards, there was less interest in the mystical lore which surrounded the sacred cup, though the study of alchemy continued to grow and in its own way kept alive the concept of the vessel. What remains to be considered in detail is the role played by the Grail in the history and beliefs of the Middle Ages, through which often dark and confused time it shines like a brilliant star.

## The Maiden Makeless: Mary and the Grail

Parallel to the flowering in Europe of the idea of Courtly Love, and subtly connected with it, was the emergence of a cult of the Virgin Mary. Reverence for the Mother of God had always been more pronounced among eastern Christians, but it was not until the crusaders, returning from the Holy Land at the end of the eleventh century, brought with them ideas which strengthened the belief, that Mary began to develop a real following in the west. Worship of womankind, extolled by the new breed of Troubadours, encouraged the pious to place Christ's Mother even higher than before – so high that in some areas Her cult began to attract more followers than Her Son's. Shrines to the Virgin sprang up across Europe, and the great abbeys vied with each other for the splendours of their Marian shrines.

Britain took the lead over the rest of Europe in this; for, as everyone knew, Joseph of Arimathaea had built the first Christian church there, and Christ Himself, appearing in a vision, had dedicated it to His Mother. A tradition so strong that Britain is still referred to as 'the Dowry of Mary'. And, with the growth of interest in the early history of the Grail, it was inevitable that a connection should be made between the story of Joseph bringing the Grail to Glastonbury, and the dedication of the first church to Mary.

In the *Queste del Saint Graal*, at the moment when Galahad enters Sarras with the Grail, the text refers to the 'Mass of the Mother of God' being sung in the cathedral; and in both *Perlesvaus* and the *Morte d'Arthur* there are specific references to the 'Mass of Our Lady' being performed at the mystery of the Grail. Indeed *Perlesvaus*, which was almost certainly written at Glastonbury, states that the Virgin took the part of celebrant at the Mass, and offered Her Son as the living sacrifice. Later in the same text we read that 'Every day our service be done in the Most Holy Chapel where the Most Holy Grail every day appeared, and where the Mother of God abode from the Saturday until the Monday that the service was finished'.

The possibility of a Marian Grail cult at Glastonbury cannot thus be ruled out. The Tor, which dominates the surrounding area, undoubtedly has ancient links with pre-Christian religious activities. It has been suggested (Ashe 1979) that there may once have been an initiatory maze cut into its sides; and if this was so, it is more than likely that the objective of the initiate, having pierced the centre of the maze, was to imbibe a draught from a sacred vessel which he would find there. Memories of such a rite, centring around the religion of the Earth Mother, could well have been revived with the appearance of the Grail romances. Ceridwen, the Welsh mother goddess figure, was herself, as we have seen, the possessor of a magic vessel, and of a semi-divine 'son', Taliesin. Nor did the similarity between the Welsh word for cauldron (*pair*) and the spelling of Mary's name (Mair), go unnoticed. The Welsh poet, Dafydd Benfras, who lived during the period of the Grail romances, wrote 'Christ mab Mair am Pair pur vonhedd.' (Christ son of Mary, my cauldron of pure descent.)

Here we possess a clue to the association of Mary with the Grail. In the mediaeval *Litany of Loretto*, the Virgin is described as

| | |
|---|---|
| *vas spirituale* | spiritual vessel |
| *vas honorabile* | vessel of honour |
| *vas insigne devotionis* | singular vessel of devotion |

referring to Mary as the vessel (womb) in which divinity had become manifest. In effect, Mary becomes a *living Grail*, containing the blood and the spiritual essence of Christ. The *Litany* makes this point even more strongly in making the Virgin

| | |
|---|---|
| *causa nostrae laetitiae* | cause of our joy |
| *foederis arca* | Ark of the Covenant |
| *turris Davidica* | tower of David |
| *turris eburnea* | tower of ivory |
| *domus aurea* | house of gold |
| *sedes sapientiae* | seat of wisdom |
| *speculum justitiae* | mirror of justice |
| *Regina prophetarum* | Queen of Prophets |

For the Grail, too, was a vessel of spirit and devotion, as it was also a cause of joy among those who came into its presence, as well as being the Ark of a New Covenant. It was also associated with a house of gold (the Grail temple) and with a chair (the Siege Perilous); while in *Parzival* it has a prophetic quality through the messages which appear written upon it.

In the full spectrum of mediaeval symbolism, Mary is Queen of Heaven, as well as mirror, vessel, house of gold and star of the sea, seat of wisdom and cause of joy; but Her supreme symbol is the rose – Rose of the World, Rosa Alchemica, Queen of the Most Holy Rose Garden, Multifoliate Rose. The rosary, signifying devotion to the Mother of the Divine Child, is arranged in multiples of five: five decades (tens) repeated three times, totalling fifteen decades – five was thus the number of Marian devotion; the rose was

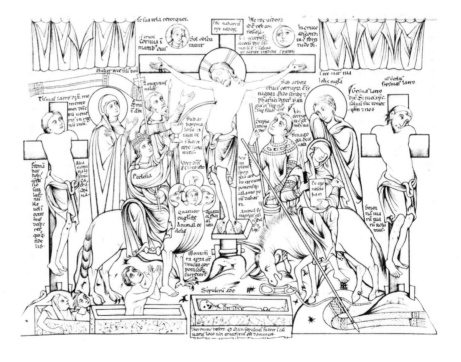

*Time stands still in this Christian mandala, as the old and new dispensations (Christianity and Judaism) assemble to witness the event of the redemptive sacrifice. Ecclesia (the Church) raises her cup to catch some of the grace-bestowing blood, while Synagoga (the Synagogue), riding on an ass, bows her head. Next to her is the lance which pierced the side of Christ. (19th c. engraving, reconstruction of Flemish 12th-c. original.)*

15

always depicted with five petals; Christ was wounded five times; and the Grail underwent five changes. And, in the elaborate symbolism of Courtly Love, the rose garden becomes the place where the beloved, the lady, the Goddess of Love herself awaits the coming of the lover who must pick the rose to achieve his desire. Dante, who fully understood the richness of the symbol, in his *Paradiso* makes the rose the image of the final revelation, granted him at the behest of St Bernard of Clairvaux, who prays for the intercession of the Virgin. For both sacred and profane, the symbol holds good.

Mary, the Theotokos, or God-Bearer, is the vessel destined to contain the spirit made flesh. With this becoming, God enters the world. In the sacrament He consents to become bread and wine. The Grail, which contains these elements, thus becomes like the womb of Mary, a house of God; and a symbol of self-fulfilment in man. As St Ephraem wrote in the fourth century, invoking Christ,

> *In the womb that bore you, are Fire and Spirit,*
> *Fire and Spirit are in the river where you were baptised,*
> *Fire and Spirit are in our baptism too,*
> *And in the Bread and Cup are Fire and Spirit.*

and again

> *Mary has given us the Bread of Rest,*
> *In place of the Bread of Toil which Eve provided.*
> (*The Harp of the Spirit.*)

Mary redeemed the sin of Eve, as Christ redeemed the sin of Adam; new light and life is contained in the Grail-as-chalice, and in this image it is at its most sacramental: a 'hallow' of mankind. In imagery such as this we find the Troubadours addressing Mary as 'Grail of the World', and applying the term with equal validity to the 'lady' of the rose garden: 'The beloved one is the heart's Grail, her lover will not be alone, for she is to him the highest Grail, which protects from every woe.' (Fisher, p. 110.)

When Mary asked, at the time of the Annunciation, 'How may these things be?', she is almost foreshadowing the question of the Grail seeker, who must ask, 'Who is it the Grail serves?' The 'who' and the 'how' are interchangeable, and the answer to both questions is Christ – as the Fisher King and as the Messiah. Mary too serves God, and through Her Son, mankind. As Angelus Silesius said, man must 'become Mary and bear God from within', before he can win truth and wisdom – just as the Grail seeker must achieve his quest in order to attain the same goals.

Joseph of Arimathaea, who built the first Marian shrine, and perhaps placed the Grail on an altar within it, shared the title *paranymphos* ('friend of the bride') with St John, and also shared the responsibility for the guardianship of the Mother of God. In this way it may be that, from being the guardian of the vessel of the Holy Spirit, Joseph became the guardian of another vessel – the Grail. (See Anderson, pp. 112–13.)

In looking at the idea *behind* the symbol, we seem to catch a glimpse of a dual natured Grail figure: on the one hand the Virgin Mother, and on the other the Grail King, who is a type of Christ – in fact, almost a uniting of Christ and Mary. It is as though, like the androgynous figures of alchemy, they represent the nature of God as a duality, male and female, anima and animus, contained within a single image of wholeness, the Grail.

## The stone vessel: the Grail in alchemy

In *Parzival* the Grail is described, not as a cup, but as

> a stone of the purest kind ... called *lapsit exillas*.... There never was human so ill but that if he one day sees that stone, he cannot die within the week that follows ... and though he should see the stone for two hundred years it [his appearance] will never change, save that his hair might perhaps turn grey.

This description has always puzzled scholars, and various attempts have been made to suggest what Wolfram meant by *lapsit exillas*. Did he perhaps mean to write *lapis lapsus ex caelis*, the 'stone fallen from heaven'? This would seem to be borne out by a further statement in *Parzival* that the stone was a jewel, an emerald which fell from the crown of Lucifer during the war between God and Satan, and which was brought to earth by angels who remained neutral. Some translators interpret the emerald as being from Lucifer's forehead rather than his crown, and have linked this with the pearl fixed in the brow of the Indian god Shiva. Called the *Urna*, this stone signified the sense of eternity belonging to the god, and is like the Third Eye with which one may see inward to knowledge and perfection. Thus, without the emerald, Lucifer is doomed to inhabit the earth as a manifestation of evil; while the stone itself becomes a fallen image which can be raised up only by the Grail quest and redeemed in the act of healing performed by Perceval in its name.

This sounds remarkably like some of the processes of alchemy; and in fact the most generally accepted derivation of Wolfram's 'pure stone' is that it is a more or less direct reference to the *lapis philosophorum*, or Philosophers' Stone, the quest for which involved the minds and energies of the mediaeval alchemists almost to the exclusion of everything else.

In spite of the fascination it exerted, the *lapis* was regarded merely as a stage in the process known as the Great Work, in which they were all involved to a lesser or greater degree. The Work itself was concerned primarily with transformation – of the base elements, earth, water, air and fire, into higher states of being; and, in terms of the spirit, the baser elements in man into similarly higher realms. The part played by the *lapis* was that of a catalyst, and its creation was the first major step along the path towards realizing the highest aims of the Work – the spiritual perfection of the alchemist and his joining with God.

One of the greatest alchemists of the day, Arnold of Villanova, referred to the *lapis* in his *Rosarium Philosophorum*, written not long after Wolfram's *Parzival*:

*Hic lapis exilis extat precio quoque vilis*
*Spernitur a stultis, amatur plus ab edoctis.*

(This insignificant stone is indeed of trifling value/It is despised by fools, the more cherished by the wise.)

(Campbell 1968/74, p. 430.)

This deliberately contradictory attitude is typical of the way in which the *lapis* was described. But what is interesting here is the echo in the phrase *lapis exilis* (insignificant stone) of Wolfram's description of the Grail stone as *exillas* (which probably means the same thing). The fact that he also says it was an emerald recalls the emerald tablet of Hermes Trismegistus, the semi-mythical founder of alchemy, on which were inscribed the first precepts of the Work.

The whole process of the Great Work was carried out in the greatest secrecy and in constant fear of denouncement for heresy or witchcraft. To disguise their activities further, the alchemists devised a detailed system of symbolism in which the various elements received the names or titles of gods and goddesses, and sometimes their personalities as well. It is possible indeed that Wolfram learned some of this symbolism and carried it over into his poem without fully understanding it; as when he says that the power of the Grail stone is the same as that which enables the phoenix to immolate itself and be reborn from its own ashes. The phoenix was frequently used as a symbol of the *lapis* and was depicted as hovering over it. It is also a symbol of transfiguration in its own right and, like the Grail, stands for spiritual renewal.

That these same spiritual qualities were subject to even wider application in terms of symbolic reference is evidenced by passages from the *Aurora Consurgens*, an alchemical work attributed to St Thomas Aquinas. Here the *lapis* is described as 'a treasure house founded upon a sure rock [which] cannot be split unless it be ... smitten three times with the Rod of Moses, that waters may flow forth in great abundance, that all men and women may drink thereof.' The imagery recalls the wounding of Christ, whose side gave forth blood and water which were caught in the Grail, and is the reverse of the episode of the Wounded King, whose hurt causes the waters of the land to dry up. Aquinas may also have been thinking of the legend of the rock used to seal Christ's tomb, which has been linked with the rock struck by Moses to bring forth water to feed the thirsty Israelites in the wilderness – an act transferred to Perceval in the Grail story, when he 'frees the waters' by healing the Wounded King.

More important still is Aquinas' statement that the stone is an allegory for the soul of Mary. He had already written that the *lapis* was rightly called 'the stone of chastity', recalling the Arabic alchemist Alphidius, who taught that the *lapis* 'mother' was 'virginal', as well as Wolfram's 'pure stone'. Now he says that it is 'ever the same and ever constant and without flaw', making an additional case for the Marian Grail symbolism examined above.

But the *lapis* is not the only object of alchemical origin which has a bearing on the history of the Grail. There is the Hermetic Vessel, the *vas mirabile*, in which the basic elements of the Great Work were mixed, as were the elements of creation in the Greek *Krater* and the *Kernos* of Eleusis. According to C. G. Jung, in his study of alchemy, the semi-mythical writer Maria Prophetissa said that 'the whole secret [of the Great Work] lies in knowing about the Hermetic Vessel'. From it was born the *filius philosophorum* (son of the philosophers), the mysterious child which in alchemical symbolism stood for the birth of wisdom from the *vas*, the uterus of the Work – the uterine nature of the *vas* (and, by extension, of the Grail, Mary's womb) being thus emphasised. The idea is even more fascinating when considered along with the suggestion that Wolfram's *lapsit exillas* reflects the words *lapis exulis* (stone of exile), used by Kaballists to signify the Shekhinah, the divine manifestation of God in the material world. The Shekhinah is the Tabernacle of the Heart, and the heart is the wounded centre of the cup – which *contains* the wounds of God and is His dwelling place in the divine blood of the sacrament. Like the exiled stone, the Shekhinah is willingly exiled from Eden along with Adam, the presence of God going with (and in) him into the outside world. There is a suggestion here of the deep-rooted urge to discover the Grail and to return with it, as did Galahad, to Sarras, the heavenly city which is like Paradise.

Returning to the 'pure stone' of Wolfram, the fact that it could be interpreted as the 'stone fallen from heaven' is particularly interesting in the light of a further instance of alchemical symbolism, in which the *lapis* was identified with the stone of Saturn. According to the myth, Saturn vomited forth the stone after mistakenly swallowing it instead of his son Jupiter. This was seen by the alchemists as a symbol of the divine nature of the *lapis*, and of its baser origin as something cast aside by the god – in other words the 'despised' stone, which had its beginning in the base elements. The stone of Saturn came to rest on Mount Helicon, the holy mountain of Greece, thus becoming a stone from heaven, which lay beyond the reach of all but a few, on top of a mountain rising from the sea – precisely the imagery of the Grail!

But there is still another stone that could have influenced Wolfram's conception of the Grail. This is the Black Stone, sacred to the Islamic religion, which stands at the centre of Mecca and towards which the faithful offer daily prayers from whatever part of the world they happen to be in. Like the emerald which fell to earth, the Black Stone was believed to have been a meteorite which fell out of the sky in the distant past. It became an object of worship until the time of Mohammed, who denounced its use as such and declared that it should be used as a source of communication with God. According to Koranic sources, it was said to have been given to Ishmael by the angel Gabriel at the time of the rebuilding of the Ka'aba, or 'cubic house', where the stone was afterwards kept. In earlier times, it was said to have represented the triple-aspected mother goddess, the Mater Dea, who with the god Hubal was offered sacrifices of blood – a fact which becomes significant when considered in connection with the Grail. Interestingly, the colour green attributed by Wolfram to the Grail stone is associated with

Venus, whose day, Friday, is the Islamic Sabbath; green is also the colour associated with the Prophet, and is therefore sacred.

Like the *lapis philosophorum* and the Black Stone, the Grail was an object of supernatural origin and activity involving the prolonging of life, the birth of a divine child, the quest for wisdom and knowledge, and direct communication with God. That the stone was perfectly capable of supporting such a wide spectrum of interpretations is further demonstrated by the way it is used in Biblical sources. In the story of Jacob, for example, who falls asleep with his head pillowed on a stone and dreams of a ladder leading directly to Heaven, it is clear; and in the Book of Revelation (2:17) is written 'To him who conquers I will give some of the hidden Manna, and I will give him a white stone [*calculum candidum*], with a new name written on the stone which no-one knows except him who receives it.' The 'new name' is that individual wholeness attained only by him who completes the Great Work, or wins the Grail. It is the key to fulfilment.

## The temple of the mysteries

The home of the Grail is properly in the uncharted country of the soul; but within the framework of the stories, an externalized form – the temple, or castle of the Grail – came to be recognized as the place where, if the quester should reach it, he might find the object of his search. And because such a place must have its guardians, there came into being an Order of Grail Knights, a king and a court, conforming to the mediaeval idea of such a place, but at the same time as remote and mysterious as the ritual object thus housed.

The name of the Grail King, and of his castle, vary from text to text, but most are in agreement as to its setting at the summit of a mountain, usually surrounded by water, and as to the name of this mountain: Muntsalvach, the Mountain of Salvation. Inevitably, attempts were made to identify the site, and though there does not seem to have been an actual Muntsalvach, there were several contenders. Of these the most generally accepted is a mountain fortress in the Languedoc area of southern France. The name of this fortress, Montségur, and its history, together with that of the surrounding country, did much to establish it in the minds of mediaeval readers of the Grail stories as a site for the home of the holy vessel. The events which brought about this identification worked in two ways: the Grail castle or temple acquired a foothold in the real world; and at the same time the Grail itself became associated with a heretical sect known as the Albigensians, named after the town of Albi where they were supposed to have originated, but who referred to themselves as Cathari, the Pure.

The ultimate origins of the Cathars are obscure, though they are known to have inherited certain doctrines from Manichaeism. This sect was founded in about AD 61 and was based on the archaic Persian religion of Mazdaism, expounded in the teachings of Zoroaster in the sixth century BC (whose own life was a perpetual striving after perfection). But the Cathar movement itself arose from *within* the established church, separating itself from the main body with an élitism borne out by its choice of name. Its beliefs were of a dualistic nature, stemming from the idea that God had remained aloof from creation (actually brought about by Lucifer), giving only a fragment of Himself to man which subsequently became trapped in matter. The Cathars, like their Gnostic predecessors, saw this as a betrayal; to them man was already dead; the 'Fall' was into the death of the spirit; and this had *not* been redeemed by the suffering of Christ – though He had come as a reminder of man's true state, and His relics, such as the Grail, were held to be sacred. But the Cathars desired to return to the world of light from which they felt they had been separated, and did not believe this could be achieved through ordinary means, such as those offered by the Church. They sought, rather, their own way, which was rigorously hard, and entailed abjuring the flesh, fasting, and living a pure life. Their priests, called Perfecti, 'perfect ones', strove to reach the highest form of spiritual life – and in so doing aligned themselves with the Grail knights, whose way of life was also exemplary and required that they remain pure in body and mind. In both the Cathar movement and the Grail quest lies the image of a company whose way of life, in reflecting the ideal of Christianity, was far removed from the state of affairs in the real world.

The corrupt administration and openly displayed riches of the Church led many people to join the Cathar movement, beginning with the literate classes who were already reading the Grail romances; gradually, as the Cathar priests went out among the ordinary people, here, too, their teachings found a firm hold. Catharism, with its insistence on the responsibility of every man for his own soul, must have seemed a bright alternative to the Church's doctrine of Original Sin. The people were being offered a new kind of freedom – that of the spirit; and they were not slow to respond.

In Languedoc and Provence, culturally the most advanced areas in the western world at that time, the new movement flourished. Here the courts were both richer and far more splendid than those of their austere northern neighbours, and the flowering of poetry, philosophy and music was the object of envy on every side. The Troubadours, who, as we have seen, provided the Grail stories with some of their most potent imagery through the cult of Courtly Love, almost certainly originated in this area, and one cannot help but compare the kiss bestowed by the Courtly lover on his lady with the kiss of the *consalamentum*, almost the only rite permitted by the Cathars, as a means of transmitting light from one to the other.

So legendary were the wealth and splendour of the southern kingdoms that Philip II of France began to look askance at his neighbour. He needed only an excuse to invade, and it was given to him finally by Pope Innocent III, who in 1208 preached a holy war against the Albigensians and set in motion one of the bloodiest crusades ever. By its end, the culture of Languedoc and Provence had been swept away, the leaders and priests of the Cathars burned at the stake with hundreds of their followers. They might have been forgotten, but for the fact that they left behind them a series of legends which grew with the telling.

One of these concerned Montségur, which had become, towards the end of the crusades, one of the last strongholds of the southern forces, a bastion of Cathar strength which refused to fall victim to the crusaders. It was said that during the siege of the fortress, one of the Cathar knights appeared on the walls wearing a suit of pure white armour, and that the besiegers fled in the belief that he was a knight of the Grail who had come against them.

This was only one of the stories which linked the Grail with the Cathars, and with Montségur in particular. It was known that the only other ritual allowed by the Perfecti apart from the *consalamentum* was a kind of mystical feast known as the *manisola*; this seems to have been the same kind of event as when the Grail passed among the knights who served it and provided them with both literal and spiritual food. Muntsalvach, the Grail mountain, was ruled over by a mysterious figure, the Fisher King; Montségur, the Cathar citadel, had as its châtelaine Esclamonde of Foix, a woman reputed to be of such spirituality and goodness that even her enemies held her in respect, and who when she died refused to believe it, but held that in fact she slept in one of the caves that riddled the mountain beneath her stronghold. It was rumoured also that among the great treasures smuggled out of the fortress before it eventually surrendered was a certain 'rich cup', said to have been used at the *manisola*. Whatever the truth of this, the Cathar treasure was never recovered. It vanished into the caves below Montségur, one of which at least is reputed to have the carving of a chalice on its walls (see Guirdham, p. 85).

How much of this was in the mind of Wolfram von Eschenbach when he came to write his Grail story is impossible to say, though it has been suggested that he may have been a Cathar himself. However, what is interesting is the source he claimed to be the origin of his book. He said that he had found the matter of *Parzival* in a manuscript, written in Arabic by a Jewish astronomer of Toledo named Flegetanis, and that this work had been given to him by a Provençal *chanteur* (singer) named Koyt. This elusive figure, of whom Wolfram tells us nothing more, has so far resisted all attempts at identification, and is generally presumed to have been an invention. However, there is no reason to believe that this was so, and if Koyt and his book did exist, much that is strange about Wolfram's description of the Grail is explained.

Apart from the fact that Toledo, the supposed home of Koyt's 'Jewish Astronomer', was the centre for alchemical activities during the period of the Grail romances, 'Provençal' was almost synonymous with 'heretic', and Provence, like Languedoc, was the centre of Catharism and Manichaean beliefs and even of Sufi teachings brought from the east via Spain and the Pyrenees. Thus it is from Languedoc, if anywhere, that the eastern elements of the story entered the literature of the Grail. Wolfram, acquiring the story at a purer stage of transmission, seems to have recognized, perhaps accidentally, its mystical nature. He added his own touches, of course, perhaps even that the Grail was a stone, but carried over the influence of eastern sources in his depiction of the world of the Grail Kings. Echoes of Cathar beliefs seem to be there also, as in the neutral angels who brought the emerald to earth.

Some sixty years later than Wolfram, but belonging to the same tradition, the German poet Albrecht von Sharffenberg (usually referred to simply as Albrecht) wrote a work entitled *Der jüngere Titurel* ('The Young Titurel')

(1270) which deals with the early history of the Grail family and in particular with Titurel, the grandfather of Parzival. Included in the poem are a number of verses describing the temple of the Grail in some detail:

> In the land of Salvation, in the Forest of Salvation, lies a solitary mountain called the Mountain of Salvation, which King Titurel surrounded by a wall and on which he built a costly castle to serve as the Temple of the Grail; because the Grail at that time had no fixed place, but floated, invisible, in the air.

Albrecht goes on to describe how the mountain was of onyx, cleared of earth on the top, which was then polished 'until it shone like the moon'. The temple was high, round, domed and had a roof of gold. Inside, the ceiling was encrusted with sapphires to represent the blue sky and studded with carbuncles for stars. A gold sun and a silver moon moved across the hemispheres by artificial means, and cymbals were struck to indicate the passing of the canonical hours. The whole of the temple was rich in gold and encrusted with jewels.

For many years this was assumed to be no more than a piece of literary artifice, until in this century scholars drew attention to an actual site which bore a remarkable resemblance to Albrecht's description of the Grail temple.

At the beginning of the seventh century AD the Persian king Chosroes II built a palace which he called the Takt-i-Taqdis, or Throne of Arches (now called Takt-i-Suleiman) on the holy mountain of Shîz, in Iran. This was the most sacred spot in his whole realm, containing a sanctuary of the Holy Fire and being the reputed birthplace of Zoroaster. Here, the kings of the Sassanian line, to which Chosroes belonged, held seasonal rituals to ensure the health of the land; and when the sanctuary was laid waste, the country did indeed seem to die; just as, in the Grail stories, the infertile state of the Waste Land was seen as a direct consequence of the Grail king's symbolic death.

From more or less contemporary sources, backed up by archaeological evidence, a description of the Takt has been put together. Like the Grail temple, it was domed, roofed with gold and lined with blue stones to represent the sky. There were stars, sun, and moon, astrological and astronomical charts outlined in jewels, balustrades covered with gold, golden stair-cases and rich hangings – all resembled the temple of the Grail. The whole structure of the Takt was built above a hidden pit in which teams of horses walked round and round causing the building to revolve with the seasons and to help with the calculation of astrological and astronomical observances. This recalls the turning castles of Celtic myth, themselves often repositaries for sacred objects, as well as the turning island upon which the Grail King Nasciens found himself, as described in Robert de Borron's *Joseph*, written over six hundred years after the Takt had been razed to the ground.

Like many descriptions of the Grail temple, the Takt stood beside a great lake, said to be bottomless – a dark, still-sheet of water filling what had once been a volcanic crater. According to Albrecht, the Grail temple had doors

*Chosroes II, builder of the Takt-i-Taqdis. (Drawing by L.I.Ringbom, Sweden, 1951.)*

23

*An early Grail King, Nasciens is transported to a mysterious turning island, reminiscent of the turning castles in Celtic mythology and Persian history. (Manuscript illustration, France, 14th c.)*

on three of its sides. Takt-i-Taqdis was approachable from only three directions, two of which echo the thirteenth-century Welsh Grail text *Peredur* (in *The Mabinogion*), one across a meadow, and the other by following a stream through a valley. The fact that the Takt was fed by two rivers and that it was surrounded by a wall, as well as that devices were installed to imitate the seasonal changes in weather, recalls the mediaeval concept of Paradise, often depicted as the home of the Grail.

When an expedition was mounted by the American Institute for Persian Art and Archaeology in 1937, its members discovered, at the site of the Takt, 'a gleaming, crust-like deposit made by the mineral waters of the lake which, particularly around the edges where it had been exposed, had taken on the appearance of onyx.' (Pope.) Albrecht, as we have seen, also described the Grail temple as standing on a bed of onyx.

Finally, there exists in the Berlin Staatsmuseum a bronze dish dating from the Sassanian period, which depicts the Takt, complete with the wooden rollers on which the building turned, and shows that the central area was surrounded by twenty-two elaborate arches – *the same number* as the lesser temples which surrounded the main room in Albrecht's Grail castle.

But how was Albrecht, writing in the thirteenth century, able to describe so exactly a pagan temple which had been destroyed centuries before? The answer is probably that he read an account of it in connection with a crucial event in Christian history, which was described in numerous works. For, in the year AD 614, Chosroes, the builder of the Takt, captured Jerusalem and carried off its most sacred relic, the True Cross, returning with it to the very temple that was to be described as the home of another sacred object – the

Holy Grail. Then, in 629, the Byzantine emperor Heraclius marched to Shîz, overthrew Chosroes and tore down the Takt, returning in triumph with the Cross. This episode was much reported, and continued to be written about and retold, with embellishments, well into the Middle Ages – where doubtless Albrecht, or some unknown predecessor, discovered it and made the translation of the site from its eastern location to one in the west. What is so surprising is the comparatively short time the Takt remained standing. In a period of no more than thirty years, it established itself as a symbol of such potency that it helped give rise to the idea of the Grail temple, distant in both time and space.

Long before Chosroes built his palace at Shîz, an ancient circular temple of the Holy Fire – worshipped by the Manichaeans – stood there, perhaps dictating the shape of the building which came after. Another, similar temple of Manichaean origin was called Kuh-i-sal-Chwadcha and was built on the lake of Hamun in Sistan – Kuh means mountain, and the whole name is strikingly reminiscent of Muntsalvach. Both places were sacred: Kuh-i-sal-Chwadcha to the followers of Mani; Muntsalvach to the followers of the Grail, itself a symbol harboured on top of a mountain. Indeed it is possible to see in the Grail legend other influences of Manichaean origin: the story of the pearl for example, in which a quest is undertaken by a poorly clad youth, seems to come close to the story of *Parzival*, also about a young hero who possesses nothing (Hannah Closs, unpublished essay).

But these temples, whether of Chosroes or the Manichaeans, are not the only sources which throw light on the origin of Muntsalvach. The Japanese Buddhist stories of the mystic mountain Meru also deserve attention. Meru is sometimes depicted as a multi-tiered mountain, surrounded by water, around which the sun and moon revolve. Here the Buddha sits enthroned with his Bodhisattvas, and the phoenix walks beneath the trees; and in another version we find the figure of the fisherman connected with the mountain, just as the Rich Fisher is with the Grail castle. A bronze mirror from the treasure of Shosoui in the Todajdshi monastery at Nara in Japan shows the mountain of Meru surrounded by an ocean in which floats the fisherman in his boat – in this instance probably an avatar of the god Vishnu, who was sometimes known as the Golden Fish, or the Fisherman of Light. Again he is the guardian of the sacred mountain, and is also its numen, or local spirit. (See Closs.)

Throughout all these examples the imagery is consistently that of a sacred place where either a valuable object is kept, or else a mysterious semi-divine ruler holds sway. Most of these sacred places are ultimately identifiable as symbols of Paradise, or as recollections of an ideal state of being. A story which combines these elements and which connects them with the Grail is that of the Priest King.


## The Priest King and the Grail

The quest for the Grail is also the quest for Paradise – this much is clear from the imagery associated with the temple and the country which surrounds it. The Grail King, or Rich Fisherman, by whichever title one chooses to call him, is also a priest, for he officiates at the Mass in which the Grail is used as chalice, and he is identified with Christ, the vessel's true King. This is one of the mysteries of the Grail that sets it apart from the established Church, in the same way as its avowedly mystical properties transcend the form of Christian interpretation in which it was bound by the western romancers who put the stories in writing. Yet behind this lies much that is non-Christian in origin. The influx of ideas and culture from the east – through the agency of the crusaders and the Troubadours who travelled with them, bringing back stories and songs that became outwardly Christianized – had a lasting effect on the shaping of the Grail legend.

Even while this exchange was taking place, the east remained a largely unknown place, a barrier to even stranger, possibly wondrous, lands beyond. Paradise, understood as an actual place, was generally believed to lie either far to the west or, more likely to the east; and when word began to filter through of the existence of a Christian realm beyond the lands of Islam, many believed this to be the lost Eden, the Garden of Earthly Delights, the Blessed Realm where grew the Tree of Knowledge and where the Fountain of Life gushed forth. As more became known of this mysterious realm, the name of its ruler was established. He was called 'Prester' or 'Presbyter' John; and he was both priest and king.

A certain Bishop Hugh of Jabala first brought news of Prester John to Rome in 1145, with an account of a successful campaign made by him against the Muslims – a fact which created a considerable stir in the west, more used to hearing of defeat at the hands of the Islamic forces. But it was not until 1165 that the west became directly aware of the great Christian ruler. In that year a letter was delivered to Pope Alexander III, which began 'Prester John, by the grace of God king over all Christian kings, greetings to the Emperor of Rome and the King of France, our friends.' It went on to describe in detail the 'position, the government, of our land, and of our people and beasts' – leaving the reader in no doubt as to the splendour and importance of this hitherto unsuspected Far Eastern Christian empire.

The description is certainly startling. The land is said to contain pygmies, unicorns and the phoenix, as well as a host of even stranger creatures. Its two rivers are filled with jewels and, as the *Letter* continues, 'In our land there is also an abundance of wine, bread, meat, and of everything that is good for the human body . . . and inside our palace there is (water) and the best wine on earth, and whoever drinks of it has no desire for worldly things, and nobody knows where the (water) goes or whence it comes.' A statement in its details very reminiscent of the abundance of good things provided by the Grail. But the description does not end there; the *Letter* continues, in imagery that could have come from any of the Grail romances, 'There is still another great marvel in our palace, for no food is served in it except in a . . . trencher that hangs from a column, so that when we sit at table and wish to eat, the food is placed before us by the grace of the Holy Spirit.' This needs only the substitution of the word 'Grail' for 'trencher' to coincide almost exactly with the stories we have been studying.

But who was Prester John, and what was the origin of the *Letter*? Various theories have been advanced – among them that he was Ghengis Kahn, or the Negus of Ethiopia, whose title, Zan, may have been mistranslated by

IOANES·PRESBR·MAX·DE·IDIA·ET·ETHIOPIA

·FVGE·SVPERBIAN·TER·
·FVGE·LVXVRIA·DELIGNO·
·FVGE·GVLAM·DEPLVMBO·
·FVGE·IRAM·DE·FERRO·
·FVGE·INVIDIAM·DECVPRO·
·FVGE·ACIDIAM·DEARGENTO·
·FVGE·AVARITIAM·DEAVRO·

PRESTO·GIOVANNI·DE·INDIA·ET·ETHIO

*John, the Priest King, a mysterious figure whose vast Christian kingdom is here said to include India and Ethiopia. A nephew of the Grail hero Parzival, he became the last earthly guardian of the holy cup. (Woodcut, Germany, 15th c.)*

French or Italian merchants as Jehan or Gianni, or read as Zanni, the Venetian for John. Another theory says that he was a Manichaean ruler named Yeh-lü ta-shi, who was also called Gur Kahn and who led an army against the Seljuk Sultan Saijar and gained undying fame as an oppressor of the Muslims. The truth is that Prester John shares the characteristics of all these figures, but there is little evidence to connect him with any single historical character. He seems to have made an almost spontaneous appearance, embodying the desires of the western world for a lost Paradisial state, ruled over by a benign and wise lord. There is evidence also, in the form of an anonymous account written some time after the *Letter*, that suggests a connection between Prester John and the Apostle Thomas, who is supposed to have travelled to India as a missionary not long after the crucifixion, and there founded the Nestorian Church, a breakaway sect of early Christians who established colonies first in Syria and then later in India and China. This contact with the Nestorians may also have resulted in Prester John's realm being identified with India.

This anonymous account describes the visit to Rome, in the year 1122, of a certain 'Patriarch John' and relates details of his ministry and homeland. He lives, it is said, in a great city with walls thick enough to drive two chariots abreast along the top of them. Through the city runs the river Physon which rises in Paradise; and a short way beyond the walls is a mountain, on top of which stands the church of St Thomas the Apostle. This mountain is surrounded by a lake, around the edge of which are sited twelve monasteries filled with pious monks. Only at certain times – a week before and a week after the Saint's feastday – do the waters sink, permitting access to the central shrine, where hangs a silver vessel from chains in the roof. In this vessel is the uncorrupted body of the Saint, which at such times is lowered from its place and the body placed in a chair – from which position, at the height of the Mass, St Thomas himself dispenses the Host from a golden dish. Those who were true believers benefited from the Eucharist; but if any heretic partook, they either repented or fell dead.

This story bears so many parallels to that of the Grail, that it is hard not to believe that it may have been an indirect source for details which appear in the romances. For here we have all the elements of the Grail story: the temple on top of a mountain surrounded by water; the vessel containing a sacred relic; miraculous events which take place regularly at the same time; the blessing received by those who are true adherents, and the dire effects upon those who are not. Even the twelve monasteries around the lake are reminiscent of the Round Table with its (originally) twelve seats. The vessel suspended by chains recalls the magic bowl in the *Yvain* story, which caused a storm when water from it was poured over an emerald; as well as the account of another very similar object to be found in the *Mabinog of Manawydan Son of Llyr*. In this story, the hero Pryderi, whom some scholars have identified with Perceval, entered a mysterious castle and there discovered

A fountain with marble stone around it, and a golden bowl fastened to four chains, the bowl set over a marble slab and the chains extending upwards so that he could see no end to them ... he walked over to the bowl and grasped it, but as soon as he did so his hands stuck to the bowl and his feet to the slab he was standing on, and his speech was taken so that he could not say a single word. There he stood.

(*Math vab Mathonwy*, in *The Mabinogion*.)

Here, once again, we have an otherworld setting; the castle which Pryderi enters, in search of a magic beast, is an image of the Celtic Paradise; Prester John's kingdom is clearly the same, being a land of plenty, with rivers that divide it into four parts and inhabited by a gentle, Christian people and curious beasts. Also it contains the Tree of Life, as well as a fountain which, if one bathes in it, enables one to live a hundred years while retaining the appearance of only thirty-two. Prester John himself says that he has bathed there six times and is now 562 years old. Again we are reminded of the Grail, the mere sight of which is enough to grant extended life.

What better place than this spiritual no-man's-land, between this world and the next, at a slight remove from reality but still 'historically' attested to, for the earthly home of the Grail, sometimes called *lapis exulis*, which has been interpreted (Campbell 1969) as the wish for Paradise? And it is precisely here that Wolfram places it, by inference if not in actuality, by making Prester John the eventual guardian of the Grail. In doing so, he is once again following his habit of borrowing from eastern sources and placing them in a Christianized framework. He shows us quite clearly that his sympathies lie with Islam, and at the same time gives his own version of Prester John's origin.

Gamuret, Parzival's father, puts himself at the service of Islam as a mercenary because it satisfies his need for perfect spiritual knighthood in a way that service to a Western lord cannot. By Belcan, a Muslim woman, he has a child named Feirefiz, who is Parzival's half-brother; it is interesting to note that Belcan is described as 'black as night', while Herzeloyde, *Parzival's* mother, is called 'clear as the light of the sun'. As Gamuret marries both ladies he is incidentally reconciling dark and light, and, by extension, east and west.

Feirefiz, though a Muslim, is made almost as noble a character as Parzival. It is astonishing that Wolfram should consider a Pagan capable of coming close to attaining a goal which many Christians could not, yet he allows Feirefiz to reach the castle of the Grail – though when the stone is carried into the hall he cannot see it; the reason being that he has not been baptized. Feirefiz has eyes only for the Grail maiden, the daughter of the Wounded King, and when matters are explained to him he says: 'Is that her God? If I accept that God, can I marry her?' (Campbell 1969, p. 221.)

On being told that he may, Feirefiz accepts baptism, the form of which is strange indeed: a font is brought in and placed before the Grail, at which it becomes filled with water – perhaps, as has been suggested, the *aqua permanens*, or Water of Life, which is at once a concept of alchemy and also of far earlier times, when the cauldron rather than the cup was the focus of reverence (see Campbell 1969). And, on the Grail, that highest point of reference outside God, a message appears; one of tolerance for other races and creeds, including, as is made clear from its place in the narrative, the Muslims: 'If any member of the Grail Company should, by the Grace of God, be given mastery over a foreign folk, he must not speak to them of his race or his name, and must see to it that they gain their rights.'

Feirefiz and the Grail King's daughter are married, and their son is – Prester John, who rules over his kingdom with a sceptre of emerald. He is thereby directly related to the Grail family, and in time becomes the guardian of the Holy Vessel. The Grail is thus transported out of this world, into the realm of the spirit, where it remains. The theme of *Parzival* is really the reconciliation of Christian and Muslim in a state which is beyond their differences – a Paradise where both can live in peace.

*The opposition of Christian and Muslim was to be reconciled through the character of Feirefiz. (Drawing of stained-glass window at Chartres cathedral, France, 13th c.)*

*Galahad, Perceval and Bors meet for the last time in this world at the table of the Grail. (Manuscript illustration, France, 13th c.)*

## The Grail within

The quest for the Grail is never truly over. As much for today as for the time when the romances were first written down, it is a symbol of great richness – though its meaning is as enigmatic now as then. Though we may speculate as to the truth of the mystery, we are less equipped than men and women of the Middle Ages. They were nearer, not only in time, to the stories and to the mystery of things, and it is to these stories that we must turn for even the most tentative elucidation.

It could be said that there are three kinds of Grail, apart from its many differing manifestations. There is the Grail of the Heart, the Grail of the Mind, and the Grail of the Spirit. The Grail of the Heart we view with our emotions, apprehending it with the essential part of our being – in the symbols of the cup and the spear. The Grail of the Mind appeals to the subjective approach, which sees the object through a penumbra of strangeness and tries to make sense of it. But the Grail of the Spirit is, now as it has always been, a beacon which draws us towards it, willing or not, until we recognize it; or until it brings a change in us, as it did to the Arthurian world.

Properly approached, however, the Grail is part of us, sets us free like the imprisoned waters which revitalized the Waste Land. Not for nothing is the wine of the Eucharist called the Spiritual Drink; in the Mass of the Grail it is more than this. For at that Mass, the fullness of the mystery is revealed. The participants saw 'emerging from the Holy Cup a naked man whose hands and feet and body were bleeding, and who said to them: "My knights, my sargents, my loyal sons, you who in this mortal life have become spiritual creatures and who have sought me out so diligently that I can no longer hide myself from your eyes."' (*Queste del Saint Graal.*)

'You who in this mortal life have become spiritual creatures.' This, surely, is the reason for the quest – this desire to penetrate the Grail of one's own being. If the answer lies in some private inner mystery, the reason for the quest becomes a need to identify the inner being with the desired goal. He who achieves the Grail is the one who succeeds in healing both a psychospiritual wound and the death-struck kingdom of the Grail King. The cup is a vessel of compassion, signifying wholeness. On his first visit to the castle, Perceval fails to ask the required question – 'Whom does the Grail serve?' – because he does not believe it to be *his* responsibility. In other words he denies its value and efficacy for himself, turning from the truth he *can* see in search of one he cannot. His failure lies not so much in omitting to ask the ritual question, as in his refusal to ask a simple, human; 'Oh King, what ails thee?' (Closs). Only by asking such a question can he identify his desire for perfection, passing the boundaries which divide him from it. In reality it is *he* who serves the Grail, and the Grail who serves *him*. He *is* the Grail. Failure to recognize this results in separation, and gives a new definition to the words *lapis exulis*. We expel ourselves from Eden. The idea is age old and records the state of humanity's division within its own soul. The breach can be healed only when the nature of the wound is identified with its source. The questions 'Whom does the Grail serve?', 'What is it?', 'How may these things be?' have to be asked anew by each quester. As James Joyce wrote, 'Any object, intensely regarded, may be a gate of access to the

The Omphalos in Jerusalem, representing the centre of the Christian world as a vessel containing a stone. (Drawing by L. I. Ringbom, Sweden, 1951.)

aeon of the gods', and we can see that such a regard can have two results. Either the object becomes a vehicle of worship, like the Torah, the Host or the Black Stone; or it loses its separate identity, and a kind of exchange takes place, as in St Paul's 'I live no longer, Christ lives in me', or in the alchemist's contemplation of the *lapis* which causes him to become one with it. The Grail knight must see his own face reflected in the cup, and understand that the way he must travel, which may well be the longest, is without mediation – it is a direct experience of God. (Caitlín Matthews.)

This is why, when Galahad sets sail for the city of Sarras, taking the Grail with him, it has gone from the sight of man forever. Sarras, like the quester once he has set out, is no longer entirely in this world from the moment when Galahad steps ashore. It is a world between two worlds, and the cup itself is the bridge. In Sarras, life in the Grail begins.

The alchemist, Arnold of Villanova, wrote: 'Make a round circle and you will have the stone of the Philosophers' (quoted in Brennan). The Grail, whether as a stone, the product of symbolic alchemy, as a divine personage, or as a cup, the container or the contained, remains at the centre of the circle; the centre which is also the circumference, and to which all quests lead. The knights in their wanderings attain the goal that would have remained inaccessible had they gone purposely to the Grail castle. In surrendering themselves to chance they are able to make their way to the heart of the mystery – where some at least recognize the truth. Their adventures are only just beginning, for only from there can the way beyond be found.

Symbolizing the spiritual goal, the rose of the enclosed garden reflects the search for Paradise, which is at the heart of the Grail legends. The flower, like the vessel, was depicted as the object of a profound search, and was kept hidden from the undevout. (Printer's ornament, 15th or 16th c.)

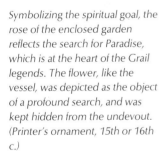

The Grail as it is most often
imagined: as the Chalice of the
Mass. The original cup, brought
from the Holy Land to the west by
Joseph of Arimathaea, was said to
have been the vessel used by Christ
at the Last Supper, and to have later
contained some of His sacred blood.
The Grail was thus linked,
symbolically, with the central
mystery of the Christian faith, and
became an object of reverence and
a sign of the truth. (The Ardagh
Chalice, Ireland, 8th c. AD.)

Beside the spring of Barenton in Brittany there was said to hang a golden basin which, if used to pour water over an emerald lying near by, would cause changes in the weather. This recalls both the Spring of Chance in the *Livre du Cueur d'Amours Espris* (see p. 61) and the alchemical Great Work, with its mercurial waters and Philosophers' Stone (which, like the Grail itself, is often referred to as an emerald).

The creation of the Philosophers' Stone and the quest for the Grail both symbolize the pursuit of spiritual perfection, also sought by the Cathars.

Montségur, in Languedoc, was an important stronghold of this heretical sect, and after its fall rumours circulated of a certain rich cup which had been kept there and which was believed to have been used by the heretics in their secret ceremonies. The carving of a cup was later found on the wall of a cave beneath the citadel. Montségur is only one of many sites – another being Monserrat, in Spain – which were centres of secret Grail worship, and so led people to give them names reminiscent of Muntsalvach (Mountain of Salvation), the legendary home of the Grail.

Joseph of Arimathaea, who is said to have brought the holy cup from the east to Britain, stands under the shadow of Glastonbury Tor, its first resting-place in this country. He is also believed to have founded Britain's first church at the spot now occupied by the ruins of Glastonbury Abbey, and to have built there a shrine for the Grail. Joseph planted his staff at the summit of Wearyall Hill, at which point it burst into flower. Scions of the Glastonbury Thorn continue to flower every Christmas, and Glastonbury has become the centre of Grail stories in Britain. (Joseph of Arimathaea, icon by a monk of the Brotherhood of St Seraphim of Sarov, England, 1978.)

Joseph is said to have received the cup from Christ in a vision, and tradition has it that the authors of the *Estoire del Saint Graal* received the story of the cup from a heavenly source. Here the Dove of the Holy Spirit descends with the book in which the story is written, while God the Father and God the Son watch from above. Uniquely, the sleeping figure is depicted as an Oriental, and the landscape is suggestive of the east. The recurrent theme of the east as the home of the Grail is developed by Wolfram von Eschenbach in particular, who (in his *Parzival*) makes Prester John its final guardian and thus reconciles the opposition of east and west. (*The Estoire Given to the Hermit*, manuscript illustration, France, 15th c.)

St John the Evangelist looks up at the crucified Christ, whose wounds are located on the Kabbalistic Tree of Life. The Tree is made up of ten Sefirot, or Divine Attributes, which together form a system of universal attribution. Here two of the Sefirot correspond to Christ's wounded side: Tiferet in the centre and Malkhut at the base of the Tree. Tiferet is the Heart of Hearts, the essence: Christ's blood too contains the essence of His spirit, the Heart of the universe. Malkhut represents the presence of the divine in matter, and is here illustrated by a cup, in which the blood of the sacrifice is given for man's redemption. The aim of the magically oriented Kabbalist is to perfect the design of the Tree by redeeming Malkhut, at present exiled from God. On the perfected Tree, Malkhut, the cup, will be transposed to the invisible Sefirah of Daat, spiritual perfection (located below Hokhmah, the eye of God, and Binah, the horn of plenty), thereby entering the sphere of God and symbolizing the redemption of mankind. This is precisely the object of the Grail quest. (Engraving, Austria, 16th c.)

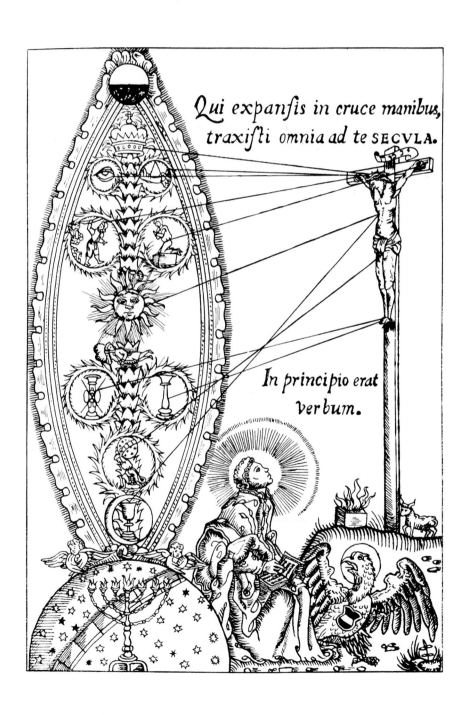

The 'Red Mass' is a stage in the alchemical Great Work, the object of which was the transformation of the base elements – in matter and man – into higher states of being. Here it is taking place in the Enclosed Garden (Paradise) and is identified with the offering of Christ, who shed His blood for man's salvation. Christ holds out chalices to the sun and moon, while more blood flows from His wounded side into the Fountain of Life, which feeds the later stages of the Work and is crowned by the figure of Mercurius, the divine child whose birth is the outcome of the Great Work. (Engraving, Germany, 17th c.)

Perceval, resting awhile on the quest, sees a vision symbolizing the old law (the Jewish religion) and the new law (the Christian Church). They are personified by Synagoga riding on a dragon (the Beast of the

Apocalypse, which represents the fallen state of mankind) and Ecclesia riding on a lion (the symbol of resurrection). Ecclesia usually carries a cup in which she catches Christ's blood shed at His Passion, the turning point from the old law to the new.

The quest for the Grail is a journey from ignorance to enlightenment, and the fact that Perceval, the Perfect Fool, is shown the vision means that, although still far from the full revelation, he is approaching the realization of his goal. (Manuscript illustration, France, 14th c.)

In Wolfram von Eschenbach's *Parzival* the knights who guarded the Grail were called Templeisen (Knights of the Temple), referring perhaps to the historical order of the Templars, who were believed to have possessed the Grail. Wagner, in his music drama *Parsifal*, from which this scene comes, gave them the same name. *Parsifal* (his last work) came as a profound expression of Wagner's spiritual ideals. Describing it as a 'sacred drama', he refused to allow its performance outside the theatre at Bayreuth, which had become a temple enshrining his work, and which for him became a kind of Grail temple also.

At a time when Tennyson's *Idylls of the King* had made the Arthurian legend an English national epic, the artists of the Decadent Movement found the dream world of the quest an attractive subject, though they endeavoured to inject into it an element of the macabre which did not exist in the original. Beardsley's Grail remains essentially a decorative motif, though, unlike his other illustrations on the theme which parody the romance and symbolism of the legend (the very elements that other artists stressed), this particular example transcends the artist's view of the image. (*The Achieving of the Sangreal*, 19th c.)

The Round Table at Camelot was the starting point for the Grail quest undertaken by Arthur's knights, many of whom never returned. Only three (Galahad, Perceval and Bors) found their way to the castle of the Grail, and only Galahad was permitted to behold its contents. Merlin, Arthur's advisor, had long before prophesied the coming of 'the Perfect Knight' who would achieve the Grail and sit in the Siege Perilous, the empty seat at the Round Table which symbolized that vacated by Judas at the Last Supper. In the earliest versions of the story, the Round Table was deliberately designed to bring this to mind. Arthur, surrounded by twelve knights, sat in the place of Christ, and Galahad, by taking that of Judas, performed a redeeming act, completing the circle at the Table, which had to be a harmonious whole before the quest for the Grail could begin. Here Galahad is shown arriving at the court before the quest, led by the hermit who seats him in the Siege Perilous. As the author of the *Queste del Saint Graal* says, 'the trial of the seat ... was proof to them of his identity. So they did their best to honour and serve him, accounting him master and lord of all their fellowship.' (Manuscript illustration, France, 12th c.; manuscript illustration, Syria, 12th c.)

45

The vessel as a symbol of spiritual transformation and renewal is to be found in mythologies far older than the stories of the Grail. In Greek myth, for example, the witch Medea proved that her cauldron could renew life by cooking an old ram in it and producing a live lamb. The hero, Jason, who was captivated by Medea, is also said to have been rejuvenated in this way, and the theme of vessel here meets that of quest, since Jason was in pursuit of the Golden Fleece. (Hydria, Greece, 5th c. BC.)

Further west, in that part of the world believed by the Greeks to be inhabited by demons, is told the

LOVVAD·SEIAO SÃCTISSIM·SACRAMENTO

Celtic legend of Taliesin, who, as the boy Gwion, accidentally tasted the brew from the cauldron of Ceridwen (a figure very similar to that of Medea) and was reborn as a great poet. (See p. 10.)

Later, acquiring the imprint of Christianity, the vessel became the chalice containing the wine that is transformed into the blood of Christ. The mediaeval clerics, however, who wrote down the Grail story looked beyond Christian symbolism to the classical and preclassical versions of the vessel as a source of spiritual renewal. (Flag of the Christians in the Shimabara Rebellion, Japan, 17th c.)

When Galahad, Perceval and Bors arrive at Sarras, the Holy City in the East, they take part in a Mass in which the Grail is used as a chalice and where the celebrant bears the stigmata. David Jones' painting, entitled A *Latere Dextro* (which, translated, means, 'On the Right Side' and is an echo of the Creed: 'Jesus Christ . . . who sitteth at the right hand of the Father'), assembles a number of images associated with the theme of man's redemption through the sacrifice of Christ, and with the symbolism of the Grail. The Paschal Lamb appears twice, once in triumph on the foreground pillar, and again, bottom right, with blood and water issuing from its side into a cup. From there, water overflows onto the ground, symbolizing its renewal, just as the Waste Land of the Grail King is revitalized by the achieving of the cup. A circle of five-petalled roses surrounds the upraised chalice, signifying the blood from the five wounds of Christ; behind the left-hand pillar, Mary, the God-Bearer, the living vessel, holds the body of her stricken son, whose agony is transcended by the action of the Mass and the figure of the priest, who bears the wounds from which light shines, pointing the way towards man's salvation and renewal. (Watercolour, England, 1943.)

The images of sacrifice which appear in the more overtly Christianized versions of the stories indicate that the Grail was meant to be seen as a symbol not only of Christ's Passion, but of the individual suffering which must be transcended before the attainment of spiritual perfection. Perceval's sister sacrificed her own life for that of a sick woman, her blood flowing into a golden cup; and it is clear that her offering is miraculous, for her body remains uncorrupted and accompanies Galahad, Perceval and Bors on their final voyage to Sarras, where it is buried ceremonially. (*The Death of Perceval's Sister*, manuscript illustration, Italy, 14th c.)

The cup symbolizes the transcendence of life and death, the passage beyond these states into a realm of higher consciousness. Narokhachöma, a Tibetan *dakini*, or goddess, drinks blood from a cup made from a human skull, symbol of the impermanence of the physical body. In various meditation practices of Tibetan Buddhism, skull cups are used, like the sacred cup of the Grail, as vessels of transformation. Sometimes associated with the goddess and her menstrual blood, the cup contains the seeds of release from the endless circle of existences. At other times the yogi imagines himself cutting up his physical body, which together with its fluids is transformed into nectar, which the gods are invited to drink at a feast celebrating his release from the ego. (Bronze statue, Tibet or Nepal, 16th c.)

A vessel containing pomegranate seeds was offered to the goddess Persephone by Hades, the Greek god of the underworld. By partaking of them as she did, she would have been forced to remain forever in Hell, had not her mother, Demeter, struck a bargain with Hades whereby she was allowed to return to earth for eight months. When she returned each year, the land, which had become barren in sorrow for her departure, flowered again – as, in the Grail stories, the Waste Land blooms again after the achieving of the cup. (Kylix, Greece, 5th c. BC.)

The central mystery of the Grail is nowhere better summarized than in the Mass performed by Josephus, the son of Joseph of Arimathaea, in the presence of the first Grail knights. Four angels are in attendance (presumably Raphael, Michael, Gabriel and Uriel), and Christ, in the image of the Divine Child, appears in the cup. On the table lies the spear with which, according to some versions, the Grail King will first be wounded, and later healed by the knight who achieves the quest. The dual themes of sacrifice and redemption are thus brought together at this early stage of the story, before the quest begins. (Manuscript illustration, Flanders, 14th c.)

In Dante's *Divine Comedy*, written in the early 14th century when the Grail legends had become widely known, the poet presents us with another kind of spiritual quest. Inspired by his earthly love for Beatrice, Dante made his work a celebration of a spiritual love, that of God for man. In this image, the white rose is a symbol of Paradise to which the souls of the blessed are admitted. (*Paradiso*, Canto 20: 31.) The rose, shaped like a cup, contains them within its petals. Like the Grail, it symbolizes the perfection sought by the knights who went on the quest and by Dante who sought the divine love of the spirit. (Manuscript illustration, Italy, 15th c.)

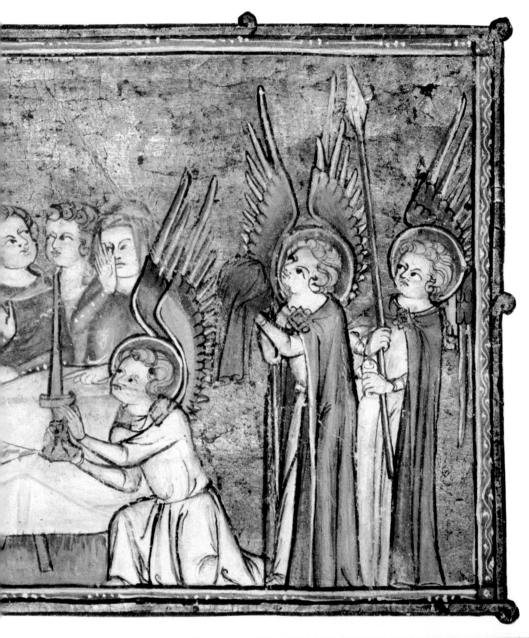

The image of the Divine Stag, an early symbol of Christ, appears frequently in the literature of the Grail – either leading those who lose their way on the quest, or even bearing the Christ Child Himself in its antlers (see p. 89).

A stag was once hunted on Good Friday by St Hubert, then still an unbeliever. When it turned, Hubert saw that it had a crucifix between its antlers. The figure of Christ spoke, asking why Hubert was pursuing him, whereupon the huntsman realized he had been seeking Christ from within for many years, and so embraced Christianity. This story parallels the quest for the Grail, which men seek in vain until the object of their search seeks *them* out, and only then reveals its fullest meaning. (*The Conversion of St Hubert*, oak panel, Germany, 15th c.)

The Mass of St Gregory the Great – who initiated the mission of St Augustine to the Saxons in Britain – depicts a miraculous manifestation of Christ during the Eucharist, which was supposed to have occurred in Rome while St Gregory was officiating. It parallels the mystery of the Grail Mass and indicates the importance of the doctrine of the Real Presence during the Middle Ages, which held that the bread of the Mass actually became Christ's body. This view was eventually endorsed by the Church, and may indeed have influenced the description of the Grail Mass itself, where Christ appears as the Host. (Painting, Flanders, 15th c.)

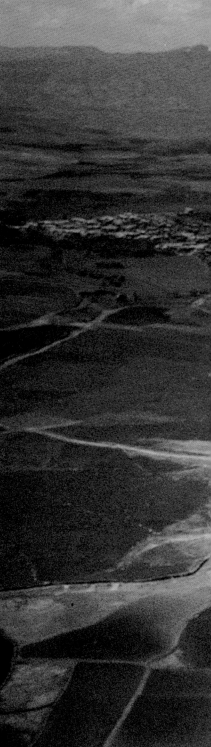

The actual site of the Grail castle has been the subject of almost as much speculation as the Grail itself – one suggestion being Castell Dinas Brân in Wales, the supposed home of the god whose name recalls that of Bron, the Rich Fisher, the first guardian of the Grail to bear the name of King. Brân also possessed a magic cauldron which could provide enough food for five hundred people, though none at all for a coward – just as the Grail provided the Knights of the Round Table, all of them brave men, with their favourite food.

Another contender for the home of the Grail is the ruined 7th-century Takt-i-Taqdis (or Throne of Arches) in Persia, built by Chosroes II. Despite its eastern setting, and the fact that it remained standing for a very short time, the Takt seems to have been the inspiration for a description of the Grail castle in a 13th-century poem, *Der jüngere Titurel*, by Albrecht von Scharffenberg, which tells the story of the first Grail Kings. The resemblance between the two buildings is remarkably detailed (see pp. 23–25). Like Albrecht's castle, built to hold the Grail, Takt-i-Taqdis was intended to be the resting place of another holy relic, the True Cross, which Chosroes pillaged from Jerusalem, and which, like the Grail, was regarded as an object of divine significance.

The theme of healing is of central importance to the Grail legend. The Grail King suffered from a wound, either in the thighs or, more specifically, in the genitals, which was caused through loss of faith or the performance of an evil act. The suffering of the king was extended to the country over which he ruled and which became barren in token of his spiritual failure. Neither he nor the Waste Land could be healed until the coming of the destined knight, who would bring new life through the achieving of the Grail and the asking of the correct question: 'Whom does the Grail serve?' The usual answer is the Fisher King himself, who was kept alive by the Grail. But there is a certain amount of ambiguity involved in the healing of the wounded king: according to the various texts, it is sometimes Perceval who heals him and sometimes Galahad, either by the Grail itself, by asking the question, or by blood from the spear which caused the wound. Here Galahad is apparently healing the king with the touch of the cup, a variant which does not appear elsewhere. (Manuscript illustration, Italy, 14th c.)

As the Grail can be said to contain healing, both of a physical and a spiritual kind, so too, the Hermetic Vessel, the *vas mirabile*, contains the elements which can cure all ills – including those of the spirit. Here, the alchemist walks through a landscape rich with the bounty of nature, which he hopes to draw forth and store in the vessel. From this, in time, will be distilled the divine essence which gives eternal life and the spiritual understanding which is the true goal of the alchemical and Grail quests. (Manuscript illustration, Germany, 16th c.)

The familiar theme of quest recurs in the *Livre du Cueur d'Amours Espris* in the search of the Heart (symbolized by the knight Cueur) for Grace, a lady of great beauty. It is set in the same sort of mysterious world through which the Grail knights roamed, and Cueur and his companion, Desire, undergo many adventures, among which is their discovery at night of a murky stream. Cueur drinks from it and pours some water back from the cup onto the stone, whereupon a terrible storm breaks. It is not until the next morning that Cueur reads the message on the slab, which promises misfortune to him who drinks, and warns of the effect of pouring water on the stone. (Manuscript illustration, France, 15th c.)

As in the story of the spring of Barenton, the theme is one of transformation, in both instances caused by the application of water. In human terms this recalls the rite of baptism which offers change and new life, and is symbolized by the fountain in *The Mystical Lamb*. The water falling into the fountain from two vessels held by the angel echoes the blood which spurts from the side of the Lamb, showing that those who receive baptism are eligible also for the redemption offered by Christ. In the Grail stories this is symbolized by the cup itself, which contains blood and water from the side of Christ, and which, through them, offers new life. (Wood panel, Flanders, 15th c.)

Only three knights out of the many who set out from Camelot achieve a sight of the sacred vessel. They are Galahad, Perceval and Bors, three very different men who experience the Grail each in his own way, and who represent three ways of approaching the mystery. For Galahad, the pure knight, is reserved the way of the Spirit, of direct communion with the godhead; for Perceval, the simple man, whose name means 'pierce-vale', the way of dedication, of the Heart, which entails a long hard road towards self-realization; and for Bors, the ordinary man, who watches the events but stands a little apart from them, the way of contemplation, of the Mind.

The three knights sail to the Holy City of Sarras, variously said to be in the east and in 'the spiritual realm', bearing the Grail to the Eucharistic celebration in which it will become at once the Grail of the Spirit, of the Heart and of the Mind. From this point there is no further that they can go. Galahad leaves the earth in a blaze of ecstasy; Perceval returns to the castle of the Grail King to become the head of the Order of Grail Knights and king of the blossoming Waste Land; Bors returns to Camelot. And, as Malory writes, 'Sithen was there never man so hardy to say that he had seen the Sangreal.' (Plate designed by James Marsh, England, 1979; *Parsifal*, charcoal drawing by Jean Delville, Belgium, 19th c.)

The true and proper home of the Grail is Paradise, the perfect realm of the spirit where the Priest King, John, its last guardian, reigns benignly from his castle within the Garden of Earthly Delights. To this place the wayfarer comes at last, leaning upon his staff, just as Perceval, Galahad and Bors came to Sarras bearing the precious cup. Here the poet comes, and the mystic, to learn and to be renewed. One of the meanings attributed to the words *lapsit exillas*, used by Wolfram von Eschenbach to describe the Grail, is the 'stone of exile' (from Paradise) and by extension the 'wish for Paradise'. Indication enough for the enlightened traveller; for the Grail is a magnet which draws all those to it who are touched by its light, and who would experience its mysteries to the full. (Manuscript illustration, France, 15th c.)

# Themes

The Grail is the spring of life, the vessel containing the promise of immortality. From it drinks the stag, symbol of the soul's thirst for God. A cornucopia, the horn of plenty and of physical renewal, is the link between the longing for immortality and the reconciliation of man's dual nature (symbolized by the two peacocks drinking from the higher spiritual cup) in the resurrection. (Stone relief, Italy 9th or 10th C. AD. Staatliche Museen zu Berlin.)

## Annunciation

The Grail, which appeared in the literature of Europe at the height of the great outpouring of mystical writing in the Middle Ages, was, like the annunciation of Christ's birth, a sign of the promise of new life for mankind.

Mary, the perfect earthly vessel, is told that she will bear the Christ Child, and the vision includes the Cross, symbol of His Passion and resurrection.

The writings of the semi-legendary alchemist, Maria Prophetissa, also spoke of the birth of a divine child – Mercurius, the product of the miraculous Hermetic Vessel. To achieve this birth, the object of the Great Work, the union of opposites was essential, here seen as the flow between two cups, upper and lower, linked by a spray of five-petalled roses, symbols of the Passion, from which comes new life. The Grail, which promises spiritual fulfilment symbolized by the blood of Christ, is the result of that Passion and its outward sign.

In Greek myth, the star represents Uranus because when he was castrated, drops of blood formed themselves into stars and were dissipated into rivers and streams. The world was thus imbued with his spirit in much the same way as the Waste Land was healed by the blood from the Grail. The *Krater* symbolized the divine matrix in which the Platonic deity mixed the elements of creation, making it a vessel of life.

The Grail is flooded with spiritual light and shines out to those who seek it. However, like the treasure at the base of the rainbow, it remains beyond man's grasp; and therein perhaps lies its continuing fascination – for modern artists and writers as much as for those of the Middle Ages.

*The Annunciation*, painting by Bartel Bruyn, German, 16th c. Rheinisches Landesmuseum, Bonn.

*Maria Prophetissa*. From Michael Maierus, *Symbola aureae mensae*, Frankfurt, 1617.

Star krater from Laconia, Greece, 6th c. BC. Louvre, Paris.

*The Wished For*. Glass engraved by Laurence Whistler, England, 20th c. Reproduced by courtesy of the artist.

## Messengers and bearers

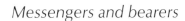

The Grail had many precursors and took many forms before it became identified with the chalice of the Mass.

This statue, from the temple at Eleusis, represents a maiden bearing the *Kiste*, in which was kept the sacred vessel of the Eleusinian mysteries, the *Kernos*, which itself contained elements of a magical drink given to initiates. Women took part in the mysteries, in the hope of bearing children; so that, like the Hermetic Vessel, the product of

which was the divine infant Mercurius, or Mary, the Mother of Christ, they may be seen as spiritual vessels for new life.

In the east the sacred vessel took different forms. It was the Jewel in the Lotus, the heart of the Buddhist mysteries, or the pearl without price, carried here by the Bodhisattva known in Japanese as Jizo Bosatsu. (Curiously, the sculpture dates from the 13th century, the period of the greatest western Grail stories.)

Maiden bearing the *Kiste*. Stone statue from the inner Propylaea, Eleusis, Greece, 4th–3rd c. BC. Eleusis Museum.

Jizo Bosatsu. Wood sculpture, Japan, 13th c.

Melchizadek foreshadows Christ in his offering of bread and wine in token of the flesh and blood of his people. He, like the guardian of the Grail, is a priest and a king. St Paul says of him that 'he is without father or mother or genealogy, and had neither beginning of days nor end of life, but resembling the Son of God he continues a priest for ever.' (Hebrews 7:3.) In the same source Christ is called 'a priest in the succession of Melchizadek' by right of his sacrifice. This statue is almost the only mediaeval depiction of Melchizadek. He is holding a cup, in which there is a stone, an image connected with the Grail, called by some a cup and by others a stone.

Joseph of Arimathaea bears two cruets containing the blood and sweat of Christ. The stained-glass window comes from Langport church near Glastonbury, where Joseph is supposed to have settled, and is the Church's only depiction of Joseph with a symbol of the Grail.

Melchizadek. Stone sculpture from Chartres Cathedral, France, 13th c.

Joseph of Arimathaea. England, 15th c.

## Messengers and bearers (continued)

Among those who bear the Grail, the central figure is that of the Virgin Mary, whose own symbols include the *vas electum*, or chosen vessel, and the enclosed garden, both of which are part of the Grail stories. Mary is the living vessel bearing the Divine Child, who is born again in the mystery of blood-from-wine in the cup. This image is akin to alchemical symbolism, in which the Hermetic Vessel is the container for the process of change resulting in the birth of the divine child Mercurius.

In the personification of wisdom as the Alma Mater crowned like a tower (Mary is the 'Tower of David'), the sacred cup contains the dew of heaven. The words around the image refer to light and to the sacred cups, the product of wisdom and of the Grail being enlightenment.

The image of the vessel occurs in the Tarot card representing Temperance. The 14th card of the Greater Arcana (the major trumps), it bears the traditional alchemical inscription 'Visit the interior parts of the earth, by rectification thou shalt find the hidden stone.' This instruction, which also appears on the emerald tablet of Hermes Trismegistus, refers both to the Philosophers' Stone and to the Grail itself, described in *Parzival* as a stone. Temperance also signifies equilibrium in the reconciliation of opposites, the revitalizing of the soul with the water of new life. She is sometimes shown – like the Grail – as bridging the gap between the inner and outer worlds. The four suits of the Tarot – Cups, Wands, Swords and Pentacles – echo the four Hallows of the Grail, which were a cup, a spear, a sword and a round platter or bowl.

*Litany of the Virgin.* Wall painting from the basilica at Lépine, Marne. France, 17th c.

Wisdom as the Alma Mater. 15th–16th c.

Temperance. Tarot card designed by Aleister Crowley, executed by Frieda Harris. England, 20th c.

Josephus, here giving the Grail to King Alain (who was converted to Christianity and became the third guardian of the Grail), was the son of Joseph of Arimathaea and it was he, according to the Grail legends, who had been the first Bishop of western Christendom, and therefore the founder of an early branch of Christianity distinct from the established Church.

The early movement away from Judaistic beliefs towards the new Christian dispensation was illustrated by the figures of Synagoga and Ecclesia. The former is blindfold, to represent those who cannot see the revelation of Christ's Passion, and carries the instruments of the crucifixion. Ecclesia bears the chalice of the Mass, the ultimate symbol of eternal life, brought by Christ's blood.

Against the backdrop of the starry heavens and the earth stand the nails of the crucifixion. Dominating the whole image is the chalice, signifying the uniting of heaven and earth in the resurrection of Christ.

Bishop Josephus gives the Grail to King Alain. Manuscript illustration, France, 15th c. Bibliothèque Nationale, Paris.

Ecclesia and Synagoga. Stained-glass panels from Châlons-sur-Marne cathedral, France, 12th c.

Angels holding a chalice of Christ's blood. Playfair Book of Hours, f.169, England, 15th c. Victoria and Albert Museum, London.

## The vessel

The Grail has had many different manifestations throughout its long history, and many have claimed to possess it or its like.

The so-called Glastonbury Bowl, a bronze vessel now in Taunton Museum, has long been associated with the centre of Grail lore, though it dates from a time much earlier than the Christian symbol.

Another cup, perhaps the best contender, and also at Glastonbury, has a long and curious history involving two people being given instructions during dreams, one to place the cup in Chalice Well and the other to find it there. Because it is considered to be sacred, it is kept purely for private worship and cannot be reproduced here.

The Glastonbury Bowl. Bronze. Taunton Museum, Somerset.

The Nanteos Cup. Wood.

The St Elizabeth Cup. Rock crystal, Egypt, C. AD 100. Staatliches Museum, Coburg.

At Nanteos, in North Wales, once resided a frail wooden cup, now little more than a sliver, since the edges have been worn away by people drinking from it in the hope of being healed (indeed many seem to have found cures). Like most of these 'Grails', it is kept hidden now, but during the 19th century it was still on view. Richard Wagner came to see it in 1855, and later wrote his great drama of the Grail, *Parsifal*, inspired perhaps by the sight of this cup.

St Elizabeth of Hungary, whose way of life reflected the purity and self-sacrifice of the Grail seeker, was devoted to the care of the poor and sick. Her father was the patron of Wolfram von Eschenbach, and so she would have heard the story of *Parzival* at first hand. After her death, her goblet was said to have performed miraculous cures upon those who drank from it.

In Jungian terms, the vessel is seen as the womb of life, the container where the constant cycle of death and rebirth takes place. The cup engraved here on a stone is a libation vessel to the unknown *genius loci*, or spirit of the place. As such, it is the offering of prayer up to God, asking for His spirit to descend to earth; these two opposite movements form the constant circle of giving and receiving between upper and lower, the human and the divine. (See also Maria Prophetissa on p. 66.)

A recent theory (suggested by Peter Redgrove and Penelope Shuttle in their book *The Wise Wound*) sees in the imagery of the Grail a symbol of the womb and menstrual cycle. There are certain details in the stories which could support this, and vessels such as this one from Classical Greece which bear symbols perhaps of ovulation, but there seems little reason to exchange the blood of sacrifice for that of physical procreation.

*Genius loci* stone. Erected by Olga Fröbe-Kapteyn, founder of the Jung Foundation, the Eranos Centre, Moscia. Italy, 1928.

Mycenean goblet from Kalymnos. Terracotta, Greece, 13th c. BC. British Museum, London.

## Sacrifice

The path of the Grail is inextricably
bound up with sacrifice: the blood of
the victim contained in the cup, which
becomes the means of healing.

Lycurgus, in a fit of madness, killed his
son Dryas, whom he mistook for a vine
stock, and his country became barren in
mourning. It was only when Lycurgus
himself was brought to his death that
the land flowered again. Beside this echo
of the Waste Land, the death of Dryas
among the vines recalls that Christ was
often referred to as a vine, and that His
blood is sometimes depicted as being
squeezed from him in a wine press.

Tizoc was an Aztec king whose name,
curiously enough, means 'Wounded
Leg'. The sacrificial stone carved during
his reign has a hollowed-out centre to
hold the still-warm heart of the victim,
offered to the god of war; from it blood
ran down the side of the stone.

The Lycurgus Cup. Glass, Egypt, 4th c.
AD. British Museum, London.

The Stone of Tizoc. Mexico, 15th c.
National Museum of Anthropology,
Mexico.

Skull cup. Silver, Tibet. Rijksmuseum
voor Volkenkunde, Leiden.

Unlike the Aztec sacrifice, that of
Tibetan Buddhism is purely symbolic.
The skull cup, which here contains the
brain, symbol of the whole
dismembered body, has many ritual
uses associated with release and
transformation. It sometimes holds,
symbolically, the flesh and blood of the
yogi himself, who transforms it into
divine nectar, which he offers up to the
gods as a release from the bounds of
bodily attachment.

74

The theme of sacrifice is shadowed by that of spiritual attainment, whether through imbibing blood or the sacred drink of Eleusis from the *Kernos*. Each of its eight cups contained one of the elements of the divine draught which, when mixed in the central bowl, opened the way to higher levels of being.

Enormous stone basins such as this one occur in tumuli all over Ireland. It is probable that the stones lying near by were put into the basins and water poured over them. The Irish shamans inhaling the ensuing steam would then be able to fall into a trance and travel the road of the spirit.

The Christian vision of the theme of sacrifice was often represented by a fish in a bowl. This stemmed from the identification of Christ with the fish by the early Christians who, in order to hide their true affiliation, used the initials of the words 'Iesous Christos Theou Huios Soter' (or, Jesus Christ, Son of God, Saviour), which together form ICHTHUS, the Greek word for fish.

*Kernos*. Terracotta vessel, Greece, c. 4th c. BC. Eleusis Museum.

Basin stone. Knowth, Co. Meath, Ireland, c. 2500 BC.

Fish in a bowl. Carved gravestone, Spain, 13th c. Lerida Museum.

## The Fisher King

The Fisher King is the guardian of the Grail, so called because the second guardian, Bron, fed his followers with a single fish from the Grail, emulating Christ's feeding of the five thousand with five loaves and two fishes.

Having received a wound which never heals, the King is kept in a state of suspended life, and the land around his castle becomes barren. Behind the figure of the wounded king is that of Christ himself, and his wound is supposed to have been inflicted by the spear of Longinus, the soldier who pierced Christ's side. The apostles were called by Christ 'fishers of men' (Mark 1:17) and Christ was represented in art as both fish and fisherman.

The Fisher King pierced in the thigh. Manuscript illustration from *Le Roman du Saint-Graal*, Ms. Add. 10,292, f.74, France, 14th c. Reproduced by permission of the British Library, London.

Jesus the Fisherman. Coptic magic papyrus, Egypt. Staatliche Museum, Berlin.

He was also identified by many with Orpheus, whose song and lyre-playing were so beautiful that the fish leaped from the sea to meet him. Like Christ, he entered the underworld and emerged unscathed, and he too was closer to his disciples than to any race or family. The crucified Christ-like figure with a crescent of stars above his head (probably the Pleiades, also known as the Lyre of Orpheus) is 'Orpheus Bakkikos' – Bakkikos because he was punished for disdaining women by being torn apart by the Bacchantes, followers of Bacchus, god of wine. Bacchus was also 'the god who relinquishes life and then is born again'

and was the symbol of everlasting life.

The Cathar cross depicts a remarkably similar figure. The Cathars believed this world to be the true hell, and that Christ in descending to earth harrowed it for them alone. They had strong associations with the Grail, and were at one time believed to be its guardians.

Poseidon, god of the sea, Hercules, and Hermes, god of voyages who also guided souls to the underworld, are all shown as fishermen, indicating the importance of the fisher as a provider of food in both the physical and spiritual senses.

Orpheus Bakkikos. Drawing by A. Becker of a seal cylinder, 3rd or 4th c. AD. Staatliche Museum, Berlin.

Albigensian cross. Stone, France, 13th c. Musée de Carcassonne.

Poseidon, Hercules and Hermes fishing. Reconstruction of a scene on a black figured Lekythos vase formerly in the Hope Collection, from J. J. M. de Witte, *Élite des monuments céramographiques*, vol. 3, 1844–61.

## Rebirth

The Grail is a vessel of initiation and rebirth. One of its predecessors is the cauldron of rebirth of Celtic myth, from which the dead emerge alive again, but unable to speak – presumably to guard against their uttering secrets learned beyond the grave. The revelation of the Grail to the knights of the Round Table was likewise accompanied by loss of speech.

The Gundestrup Cauldron illustrates the theme of rebirth in the procession of warriors killed in battle, waiting for the god Cernunnos to bring them back to life by dipping them head first into his cauldron. This same image occurs again in a much later Biblical illustration of an angel baptizing a soul, which is thereby reborn into new spiritual life.

The Gundestrup Cauldron. Silver-gilt, Denmark, 2nd or 1st c. BC. National Museum, Copenhagen.

Baptism scene. Manuscript illustration, Catalonia, 6th c. AD. Ms. Lat. 6 III, f.91v. Bibliothèque Nationale, Paris.

Ceres, goddess of fertility, bears a torch and a dish containing sprouting ears of corn. The two together symbolize the fecundation of darkness by the light of the sun, moon and stars. In the Catholic consecration of the font, the celebrant dips a lighted candle into the font and says 'May a heavenly offspring, conceived in holiness and reborn into a new creation, come forth from the stainless womb of this divine font.'

The image of the earth mother as womb, container for new life, and that of the font, which holds the water of life, are drawn together in the baptismal stoup from Herefordshire.

From the hermetic water of life is born Mercurius, crowning the achievement of the Great Work after its many processes of change.

Ceres. Fresco from Pompeii, Italy, before AD 79. National Museum, Naples.

Baptismal stoup. Stone, England, 12th c.

Mercurius in the vessel. From Johann Conrad Barchusen, *Elementa Chemiae*, Leiden, 1718.

## Circles of infinity

The most basic concept of the human imagination is the circle. It figures in the earliest cave paintings, and it is carved on the standing stones where man worshipped, themselves set up in circles.

In the Middle Ages, the sky was seen as a dome, in which the constellations moved, circling the earth and, in the zodiac, acting upon the fates of those below. Grail imagery appears in a zodiac from Lars Ivar Ringbom's book (see pp. 82–83), the Grail castle being the centre of the world, surrounded by water. The moon is in Cancer, its home,

whose stone is the emerald (Wolfram described the Grail as an emerald). Cancer is also the sign where the divine soul enters the world, just as the Grail appears to the knights at Camelot. The moon also spans Gemini, the sign of opposites, but the sun is in Libra, bringing equilibrium between the earthly and spiritual sides of man.

The Chinese represented the heavens as a disc with the symbol *pi* as long ago as the 8th century BC. The earth, *t'sung*, was a square vessel illustrating the supposed shape of the world. The union

of heaven and earth, masculine and feminine, spirit and vessel, brings perfection.

The Swinside stone circle. Cumbria, England.

The Grail temple at the centre of the zodiac. Drawing from Lars Ivar Ringbom, *Graltempel und Paradies*, Stockholm, 1951.

*Pi*. Carved jade, China, Chou Dynasty, 8th c. BC. Seattle Art Museum.

When the Grail passed through the kingdom of Arthur, strange events followed in its wake; one of its sudden appearances to the knights of the Round Table announced Galahad's arrival and his miraculous ability to draw the sword from the stone and to sit in the Siege Perilous with no disaster befalling him. The Round Table was designed as a circle to echo the circle of the heavens, with the Grail as its mystic centre.

The circular shape of the skull contains the consciousness and vital force, which is also symbolized by the genitals (when the Fisher King is wounded he loses his life force). A Tibetan skull mounted and provided with a lid is used as a ritual object, symbolically containing human blood or other vital substances of the body. The aim of the meditator is to attain *nirvana* by renouncing attachment to life and all desire (symbolized by the use of the skull), just as the apotheosis of the Grail quest is the death of the physical body and the rebirth of the spirit into everlasting life.

Galahad comes to the Round Table. Manuscript illustration from *Le Livre de messire Lancelot du lac*, Ms. Fr. 120, f.544v. France, 14th c. Bibliothèque Nationale, Paris.

*T'sung*. Jade, China, early Han Dynasty, 206 BC–AD 220. Seattle Art Museum, Eugene Fuller Memorial Collection.

Skull cup. Gilt bronze, China, 18th c. Musée Guimet, Paris.

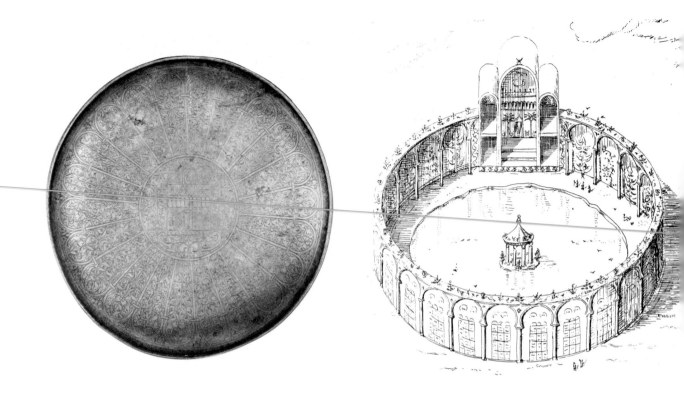

## Grail and temple

So long as it remained on earth, the Grail required a home, and because of its spiritual nature, that place was a temple. The history of the Grail temple is a complex one, involving many different images, among them that of the earthly Paradise.

In 7th-century Persia the Sassanian king Chosroes II built a temple worthy of housing the relic of the True Cross which he captured from Jerusalem. Its modern name is Takt-i-Suleiman, but he named it the Takt-i-Taqdis, or Throne of Arches (it had twenty-two arches); the bronze tray is almost certainly a representation of it.

It was not until the middle of the 20th century that the Takt was linked with the Grail temple, when Ringbom put forward the theory that it was the model for Albrecht's Grail temple in *Der jüngere Titurel* (see pp. 23–24). From the design on the tray Ringbom made a sketch of the temple, and also provided a map showing the Takt (following the concept of the Grail temple as Paradise) as the centre of the world, built on top of a hill with a river running round it and enclosed (here by mountains).

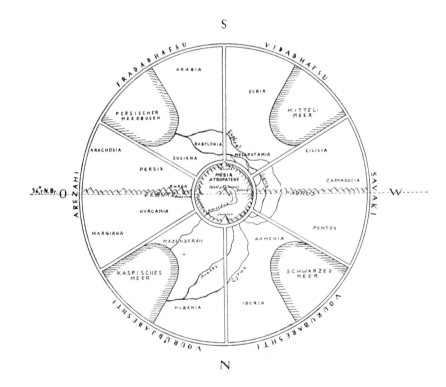

Bronze tray. Persia, Sassanian period. Staatliche Museum, Berlin.

Takt-i-Taqdis at the centre of the world. Map from Ringbom, *Graltempel und Paradies*.

Takt-i-Taqdis. Drawing from Lars Ivar Ringbom, *Graltempel und Paradies*, Stockholm, 1951.

The painting of the Grail temple as designed for *Parsifal* (see also p. 42) bears a strong similarity to the Takt-i-Taqdis with its numerous arches and the altar of the Grail at the centre.

The architect Sulpice Boisserée reflected the spirit of the 18th century in his desire to design the perfect building, but departed from it in his choice of subject (his contemporaries knew and cared little of the Grail legend), demonstrating that the Grail had not been forgotten even in that age of enlightenment.

*The Temple of the Grail.* Oil painting by Max Brückner based on set design for Wagner's *Parsifal*, 19th c.

The Dome of the Grail, elevation and ground plan by Sulpice Boisserée, France, 18th c.

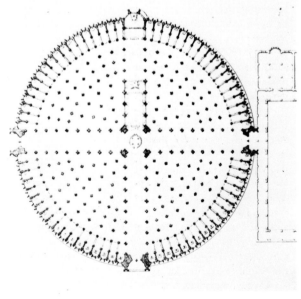

Table of the Last Supper. Manuscript illustration from the *Codex Purpureus Rossanensis*, f.3r., 6th C. AD. Rossano Cathedral.

The Table of the Grail. Manuscript illustration from Gaultier Moap, *Messire Lancelot du lac*, Ms. Fr. 112, f.3v., France, 15th C. Bibliothèque Nationale, Paris.

Galahad in the Siege Perilous. Manuscript illustration from *Li Roumans du bon chevalier Tristan*, Ms. Fr. 99, f.563r. France, 15th C. Bibliothèque Nationale, Paris.

There were three tables associated with the Grail: the Table of the Last Supper, the table at which the guardians of the cup first sat, and the Round Table of King Arthur and his knights. According to tradition, all three were round, and those who sat at them were dedicated to the seeking of spiritual wholeness.

The Grail appeared at King Arthur's Round Table 450 years after Christ's Passion, on the feast of Pentecost, the day predicted for the arrival of Galahad. In the presence of the Grail he is ushered in, and all the knights lose the power of speech. In the Bible, Pentecost was the day when the disciples suddenly 'began to speak in other tongues, as the Spirit gave them utterance'; they were enlightened in the same way as the knights were by the coming of Galahad (realizing that the Waste Land would be healed along with the Fisher King). At the Pentecostal table, tongues of fire radiate out to the disciples just as rays of light from the Grail stream down to the knights.

The Table of Belenus was intended for offerings to the Celtic god, who was slain and reborn, causing the death and rebirth of the land, in the same way as the wounding and healing of the Fisher King affected the land around his castle.

The Table of Pentecost. Manuscript illustration from *Codex Latinus*, 15713 f.37v., 12th c. Staatsbibliothek, Munich.

Offering table of Belenus. Musée Borély, Marseille.

# Voyage

The quest for the Grail is a voyage towards enlightenment and everlasting life. The stories abound in mysterious vessels which move without need of wind or tide, arrive suddenly and as abruptly depart, carrying the knights and their companions to strange harbourage and fresh adventure. In the cover picture the quest is symbolized by the knight Cueur (the heart) setting forth in just such a craft, accompanied by Confidante and Accord, for the island Paradise of the god of Love. (From *Le Livre du Cueur d'Amours Espris*.)

Galahad, Perceval and Bors, near the end of their quest, set sail in a magical craft which once belonged to Solomon and which now bears the bleeding Grail spear and the body of Perceval's sister (who gave her lifeblood to save a dying lady). Her uncorrupted corpse accompanies them on their voyage to Sarras, the City of the Grail.

The Ship of Fools is a parody of the voyage of enlightenment; it sails endlessly wherever the wind takes it. The Grail knights, however, are guided by the power of the Holy Cup, the vessel within the vessel (see p. 62). The living vessel, Mary, is herself shown bearing the Christ Child in a ship.

Perceval's sister. Manuscript illustration from *Codex Pal.* 556, 15th c. Biblioteca Nazionale, Florence.

The Ship of Fools. From an enlarged edition of *The Shyppe of Fooles*, Paris, 1500.

The Madonna as ship. Miniature from a psalter of unknown origin, Yugoslavia. Formerly in the National Library of Belgrade.

The voyage of the solar hero on the sea is a common theme in world mythology. One of the most famous heroes was Hercules who, in order to reach the island of Erytheia and steal the cattle of Geryoneus, borrowed the great gold cup from Helios, the sun god, who used it every evening to reach the east across the ocean.

For many, the destination of the spiritual voyage was Paradise, the realm of Prester John and of the Grail. The Garden of Eden, where man fell from Paradise, is shown as a vessel, wavering between heaven – represented by an angel in a castle – and the gaping jaws of hell.

Hercules. Black figured Attic vessel, style of Douris, 5th c. BC. Museo Etrusco Gregoriano, Vatican.

Paradise as vessel. From Wynandus de Stega, *Adamus colluctancium aquilarum*, Codex Pal. Lat. 412, 15th c. Vatican Library.

87

## Quest for the Grail

The beginning and end of the quest are defined moments. Between these two points lies a world of strange adventure, wonder and mystery.

To reach the temple of the Grail, the knights who set out from Camelot must undergo many tests and experience terrible ordeals. But often, when the way seems darkest, the enigmatic white stag or a hermit figure appears, to lead them forward through the mazes of forest and hill. In mediaeval iconography the stag was identified with Christ and the soul's thirst for God, which accounts for its appearance in this context (it is also accompanied by lions, symbols of Christ's resurrection).

In the arched temple, the Grail stands under a canopy, which can be interpreted as signifying sovereign power, here that of Christ who descends in his blood from the heavens (the dome) to the Grail (the chalice of the Mass) placed on the altar – the whole being the aim of the quest.

The divine stag. Manuscript illustration from the *Estoire du Saint Graal*, Ms. Brussels 9246, f.164r, 15th c. Bibliothèque Royale, Brussels.

Altar of the Grail. Illustration by Edward Burne-Jones for frontispiece of *The High History of the Holy Graal*, London, 1898.

Lancelot at Corbenic. Manuscript illustration from Codex Pal. 556, 15th c. Biblioteca Nazionale, Florence.

Perceval, Galahad and Bors achieve the Grail. Manuscript illustration from Gaultier Moap, *Messire Lancelot du lac*, Ms. Fr. 112, f.179v., France, 15th c., Bibliothèque Nationale, Paris.

Lancelot, approaching the Grail castle, sees a vision of a white stag borne up by angels with the Christ Child between its antlers, indicating his closeness to the spiritual realm.

Once the three knights have arrived at the Grail castle, they take part in a Mass at which, for the first time, they can look upon the cup unveiled.

## Grail and stone

Lully, lulley, lully, lulley;
The faucon hath born my mak away.
                    (mak = mate)

He bare him up, he bare him down,
He bare him into an orchard brown.

In that orchard there was a bed;
It was hanged with gold so red.

And in that bed there lieth a knight,
His woundës bleeding day and night.

By that bedes side kneeleth a may,
And she weepeth both night and day.
                    (may = maid)

And by that bedes side there standeth a
    stone,
'Corpus Christi' written there-on.

This mysterious mediaeval song, *The Corpus Christi Carol*, is filled with references to elements of the Grail legend: the bed with the wounded knight (the Fisher King), the weeping maiden (Mary), the brown orchard (the Waste Land) and the identification on the stone of the wounded figure as Christ. The Grail itself was described by Wolfram as a stone and as an emerald from the crown of Lucifer which fell with him from heaven and from which the cup was later carved.

The Black Stone of Mecca, too, was declared by Mohammed to be a vehicle for communication with God. He blessed the stone before it was carried into the Ka'aba, where it was to remain. For Muslims, the Ka'aba is the centre of the world, as the Grail was for the knights who sought it (see also pp. 82–83).

*Corpus Christi*. Scraperboard by Meinrad Craighead, England, 1980. (Reproduced by courtesy of the artist.)

The Black Stone. Manuscript illustration from Arabic Ms. O¹. 20, f.45r., 14th c. Edinburgh University Library.

Mecca as the centre of the world. Manuscript illustration from Arabic Ms. Ar. 2278, f.2v., 16th c. Bibliothèque Nationale, Paris.

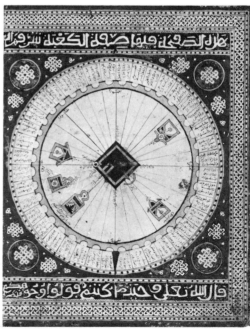

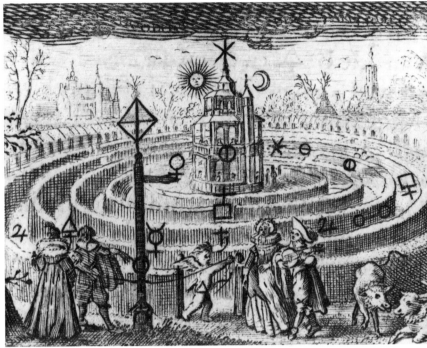

The castle of the jewel. Manuscript illustration from *Speculum Humanae Salvationis*, Ms. Lat. 511, 14th c. Bibliothèque Nationale, Paris.

The Lapis sanctuary. From Goosen van Vreeswick, *De Groene Leeuw*, Amsterdam, 1674.

For the alchemists the creation of the Philosophers' Stone, or *lapis philosophorum*, was a key stage in the Great Work. The *lapis* was sometimes portrayed as an emerald hidden in a castle, or at the centre of a maze to which only the initiated held the key. Here Death reveals the solar stone (stone of light), hidden in the earth at the bottom of a hill, exactly as the Grail is shown in the modern icon of Joseph of Arimathaea (see p. 36).

Death revealing the solar stone. Frontispiece from P. M. von Respurs, *Besondere versuche vom mineral geist*, Leipzig, 1772.

## Alchemy

The basis of the alchemical Great Work
was the reconciliation of opposites, the
creation of divine harmony in heaven
and earth, the practical and symbolic
working out of the dictum 'as above, so
below' inscribed on the emerald tablet
of Hermes Trismegistus, the semi-
mythical founder of alchemy. Perhaps
because of this tablet being described as
an emerald, as was the Grail, a link was
forged between the stories of the mystic
vessel and the process of alchemy.
Alchymya, the personification of
alchemy, here carries the Hermetic
Vessel, in which the Work takes place.
Like the Grail, it was supposed to
contain the key to all the mysteries.

War in Heaven. From *Les Prophécies de
Merlin*, Paris, 1498.

Alchymya. From L. Thurneisser zum
Thurn, *Quinta Essentia*, Munster 1570.

92

The mystic marriage of sun and moon is essential to alchemy and appears in Fuchs' *Conception of the Unicorn,* an allegory for the Immaculate Conception (the unicorn being the feminine principle, the vessel, associated with the moon as the lion is with the sun, and also representing perfect good).

The alchemical union of sun with moon is combined with the birth of the phoenix, triumphing over time. In *Parzival,* the most alchemical of the Grail texts, the power of the Grail is specifically said to enable the phoenix to live again; the alchemists believed that the *lapis philosophorum,* like the Grail, could cure all sickness and would grant eternal life and youth to him who possessed it.

In the image of the secret content of the Hermetic Vessel, the fisher appears once more, endlessly repeated within the successive circles of the search for truth; leading always towards the centre, the point where the mystery of the Grail, or stone, raises man to union with the divine.

## Attainment

The final revelation of the Grail is a coming together and offering up of all things to the higher state of being – the basic aim of most mystics.

The goddess Kuan Yin rises from the centre of the Lotus, the flower which symbolizes union in perfection, with her vase of 'sweet dew', the magical drink of those who reach the summit of the quest: Galahad come at last to the place of the Grail, the heart-centre of the search for God in the infinite.

From this point the mystery of the vessel can be expressed only in semi-abstract terms, in the Tibetan 'seed-syllable', for example, which represents the *siddha*, or 'accomplished' form of Vairocana Buddha. As the symbol replaces the master's actual image, so the Grail, to which the dove of heaven descends, is a mandala for the figure of Christ, the light that was promised, the bridge between higher and lower, earth and sky, man and God, the temporal and the infinite.

Galahad achieving the Grail. Manuscript illustration from Gaultier Moap, *La Quête du Saint Graal et la mort d'Arthur*, Ms. Fr. 343, f.18r., France, 15th c. Bibliothèque Nationale, Paris.

Kuan Yin rising from the Lotus. Gilt bronze statue, Liao Dynasty, China, 12th c. British Museum, London.

Seed-syllable A representing Vairocana. Painted scroll, Japan, 15th c. Museum of Fine Arts, Boston.

Dove of heaven descending to the Grail. Tomb of Archbishop Theodore, carved stone, Italy, 6th c. AD. S. Apollinare in Classe, Ravenna.

# Acknowledgments

*The objects shown in the text and plates, pp. 4–64, are in the following collections and publications.*

*Collections* Abbaye de Saint-Bavon, Ghent 61; author's collection 36; Bibliothèque de l'Arsenal, Paris 52–3; Bibliothèque Nationale, Paris 12 (Ms. Fr. 112, vol 3, f.15v), 40–41 (Ms. Fr. 343, f.28v), 45 (Ms. Fr. 343, f.3), 49 (Ms. Fr. 329, f.59v), 59 (Ms. Fr. 343, f.103), 64 (Ms. Fr. 1586, f.103); Bibliothèque Royale Albert 1er, Brussels 37 (Ms. Brussels 9246, f.2); British Library, London 7 (Ms. Add. 10,294, f.66v), 24 (Ms. Add. 10,292, f.22v), 44 (Ms. Add. 7169, f.11), 53 (Ms. Yates Thompson 36, f.185), 58 (Ms. Harley 3469, f.4); British Museum, London 46, 51; Galerie Marco Polo, Paris 50; Musées Royaux des Beaux-Arts, Brussels 55;

National Gallery, London 54; National Museum of Ireland, Dublin 33; Okuyama Dinshi Collection, Japan 47; Österreichische Nationalbibliothek, Vienna 60; Universitätsbibliothek, Bonn 30.
*Publications* H. Bayley, *A New Light on the Renaissance* (London 1909) 31; Sir Thomas Malory, *Le Mort d'Arthur* (London 1894) 43; Giuliano Dati, *Treatise on the Supreme Prester John* (c. 1495) 27; Herrad von Landsperg, *Hortus Deliciarum* (Strasbourg 1879) 3; *Liber Sacrosancti Evangelii de Iesu Christo Domino e Deo Nostro* (Vienna 1555) 38; Steffan Michelspacher, *Cabala, Spiegel der Kunst und Natur in Alchymia* (Augsburg 1616) 39; Lars Ivar Ringbom, *Graltempel und Paradies* (Stockholm 1951) 23, 31.
*Photographs were supplied by* ACL 55, 61; Alinari 79 above l., 95 below; Archives Photographiques 71 below l., 81 below r.; L'Atelier Art Editions,

London 62 (scene on plate painted by James Marsh for 'The King Arthur Plates', commemorative collection commissioned by the International Arthurian Society, crafted by Royal Worcester, © L'Atelier Art Editions 1979); Roloff Beny 57; Janet and Colin Bord 56; Commissioners of Public Works in Ireland 75 above r.; Louis Couvert 34; Edouard Fiévet 69 l.; Giraudon 68 r.; John A. Glover 80 above; Sonia Halliday 69 r.; Hannibal 68 l.; G.P. Herbert (courtesy Laurence Whistler) 67 below; Hurault-Viollet 70 above; Marburg 85 above; Mas 75 below; National Monuments Record 79 above r.; Piccadilly Gallery, London 63; Somerset and County Museum, Taunton (courtesy the Glastonbury Antiquarian Society) 72 above; *This England* 72 centre; John Webb © and reproduced by permission of the Trustees of the David Jones Estate) 48; Yan 35, 77 above r.

# Sources and further reading

TEXTS
'Acts of Pilate' and 'The Gospel of Nicodemus' in: *The Apocryphal New Testament* (trs. M.R. James), Oxford University Press, 1924.
*Aurora Consurgens, Attributed to Thomas Aquinas,* Marie-Louise von Franz, Routledge and Kegan Paul, London 1966; Princeton University Press, 1966.
*Conte del Graal (Perceval),* Chrétien de Troyes (ed. F. Lecoy), Champion, Paris 1975. Trs. by R.W. Linker as *The Story of the Grail,* University of North Carolina Press, Chapel Hill 1952.
*Joseph d'Arimathie,* Robert de Borron, c. 1190. Ed. by W. A. Nitze as *Roman de l'Estoire dou Graal,* Classiques Français du Moyen Age, Champion, Paris 1927.
*Jüngere Titurel, Der,* Albrecht von Scharffenberg, 1270. Repr. Augsburg 1477 (?). Parts trs. by Arthur Upham Pope in 'Persia and the Grail', *The Literary Review* (USA), I (1957), pp. 57–71.
*Letter of Prester John, The* (*Commentatio 'de epistola, quae sub nomine presbyteri Johannis fertur' . . .*), Academia Lipsiensis, Edelmanni, Leipzig 1874. Trs. from the Latin with notes by Vsevolod Slessarev as *Prester John: The Letter and the Legend,* University of Minnesota Press, Minneapolis 1959.
*Mabinogion, The* (trs. from the Welsh by Jeffrey Gantz), Penguin, London and New York 1976.
*Morte D'Arthur, Le,* Sir Thomas Malory, Penguin, London 1969; New York 1970.
*Parzival,* Wolfram von Eschenbach, 1207, in: *Parzival and Titurel* (ed. E. Martin), Darmstadt 1900–03. Trs. by

Helen M. Mustard and Charles H. Passage as *Parzival,* Vintage Books, New York 1961.
*Perlesvaus, c.* 1225: *Perceval le Gallois, ou le Conte du Graal,* pt 1, Société des Bibliophiles Belges, Mons 1866–71. Trs. By Sebastian Evans as *The High History of the Holy Grail* (with illustrations by Burne-Jones), J.M. Dent, London 1898; Attic Press, Greenwood 1969.
'Preiddeu Annwn' in: R.S. Loomis, *Wales and the Arthurian Legend,* ch.9, University of Wales Press, Cardiff 1956; Folcroft Library Editions, Folcroft 1956.
*Queste del Saint Graal: The Vulgate Version of the Arthurian Romances* (ed. H. Oskar Sommer), 7 vols, Carnegie Institution, Washington D.C. 1909–16. Relevant parts available in English are *The Tale of Balin* (trs. David E. Campbell), Northwestern University Press, Evanston 1972, and *The Quest of the Holy Grail* (trs. P. Matarasso), Penguin, London and New York 1969.
*Romance of Perceval in Prose, The. A Translation of the E Manuscript of the Didot Perceval,* Dell Skeels, University of Washington Press, Washington D.C. 1966.

CRITICAL WORKS
Anderson, Flavia, *The Ancient Secret,* Gollancz, London 1953.
Ashe, Geoffrey, *The Glastonbury Tor Maze,* At the Foot of the Tree, Glastonbury 1979.
—, *King Arthur's Avalon: The Story of Glastonbury,* Collins, London 1957; Dutton, New York 1958.
Brennan, Martin, *The Boyne Valley Vision,* Dolmen Press, Dublin 1980.

Campbell, Joseph, *The Flight of the Wild Gander,* Regnery/Gateway Editions, South Bend 1969.
Closs, Hannah, 'The Meeting of the Waters', *The Aryan Path,* Bombay, May-June 1948.
Ephraem, Saint, *The Harp of the Spirit,* (trs. from the Latin by S. Brock), Fellowship of St Alban and St Sergius, London 1975.
Every, George, *Christian Mythology,* Hamlyn, London 1978.
Fisher, Lizette A., *The Mystic Vision in the Grail Legend and the Divine Comedy,* AMS Press, New York 1966.
Guirdham, Arthur, *The Great Heresy,* Spearman, St Helier 1977.
Jung, Emma, and Marie-Louise von Franz, *The Grail Legend* (trs from the German), Putnam, New York 1970; Hodder and Stoughton, London 1971.
Mead, George Robert Stow, *Orpheus,* Watkins, London 1965; Barnes and Noble, New York 1965.
Pole, Wellesley Tudor, *My Dear Alexias* (ed. Rosamond Lehmann), Spearman, St Helier 1980.
Ringbom, Lars Ivar, *Graltempel und Paradies,* Stockholm 1951.
Wilkins, Eithne, *The Rose-garden Game: The Symbolic Background to the European Prayerbeads,* Gollancz, London 1969; Herder and Herder, New York 1969.
Williams, Charles Walter Stansby, *The Image of the City* (ed. Anne Ridler), Oxford University Press, London and New York 1958.
—, and C.S. Lewis, *Taliessin through Logres, Region of the Summer Stars, The Arthurian Torso,* Eerdmans, Grand Rapids 1974.